Roadmap
to the
Virginia SOL
EOC Biology

educators.princetonreview.com

Roadmap
to the Virginia SOL
EOC Biology

by
Michelle Rose

Random House, Inc.
New York

www.randomhouse.com/princetonreview

This workbook was written by The Princeton Review, one of the nation's leaders in test preparation. The Princeton Review helps millions of students every year prepare for standardized assessments of all kinds. The Princeton Review offers the best way to help students excel on standardized tests.

The Princeton Review is not affiliated with Princeton University or Educational Testing Service.

Princeton Review Publishing, L.L.C.
160 Varick Street, 12th Floor
New York, NY 10013

E-mail: textbook@review.com

Published in the United States by Random House, Inc., New York.

ISBN 0-375-76443-7

Content Editor: Robert Elstein
Design Director: Tina McMaster
Art Director: Neil McMahon
Production Editor: Jennifer Pollock
Production Coordinator: Robert Kurilla

Manufactured in the United States of America

9 8 7 6 5 4 3 2 1

CONTENTS

INTRODUCTION

THE END OF COURSE EXAMS

The end of what? Well, it's not the end. The End of Course (EOC) exams are only the final exams for certain "core" courses offered at your school. The Virginia Department of Education (VDOE) has decided that there are certain skills that it wants you to have when you graduate high school. Therefore, in order to receive a diploma, you must pass six EOC exams. EOC exams are given in the core subjects: English, math, science, and history and social science. These exams evaluate not only what you have learned, but also how well your school has taught its students.

WHAT EXACTLY IS AN SOL?

You've probably heard the EOC exams referred to as the "SOL tests." SOL stands for Standards of Learning, which is simply the name for the specific set of skills that the VDOE has earmarked for each core subject.

For example, in biology, the Standards of Learning state that a student should be able to understand the processes of photosynthesis and respiration. So, rather than just taking your biology teacher's word for it, the VDOE has drawn up its own exam to make sure that you do understand the processes of photosynthesis and respiration (among other skills).

If you're feeling a little nervous, don't sweat it. This book is going to ensure that you have mastered every skill that the VDOE expects you to know for the EOC Biology test. It will give you practice questions and explain the ins and outs of the test, and it will explain how many questions you need to get right and how many SOL exams you need to pass in order to receive your diploma. In short, you've purchased the only guide to the EOC Biology exam you'll ever need. Congratulations for thinking ahead!

> **TIP:** If you want to know more about the VDOE standards, try the VDOE Web site: http://www.pen.k12.va.us/VDOE.

WHO IS THE PRINCETON REVIEW?

The Princeton Review is one of the world's leaders in test preparation. We've been preparing students for standardized tests since 1981 and have helped millions reach their academic and testing goals. Through our courses, books, and online services, we offer strategy and advice on the SAT, PSAT, SAT IIs, and the TerraNova, just to name a few. The Princeton Review has created nearly twenty books to help Virginia students with their SOL exams.

WE HAVE THE INSIDE SCOOP

The EOC Biology exam is not immune to strategy and preparation. This book includes all the information about the exam you'll need to do well. The Princeton Review has been looking at standardized tests like the EOC Biology exam for years, and we'll share our special techniques to approaching standardized tests and biology questions, so you'll have every possible opportunity to score your best on this exam.

One of the biggest obstacles for students in standardized testing is test anxiety.

> **TIP:** We have made sure that every skill listed by the Standards of Learning is reviewed and practiced in this book.

Taking the EOC exams with your diploma on the line can create stressful conditions. In order to reduce stress and prepare you for this exam, we've dedicated countless hours of research to help you do well on the EOC Biology exam. In addition, we've written two practice tests to help you realistically evaluate your skills.

HOW IS THIS BOOK ORGANIZED?

This book has two primary purposes. First, we will familiarize you with the structure of the exam and recommend the soundest test-taking strategies to maximize your score.

Second, we want to make sure that you're familiar with the raw material of the exam—the actual biology skills and concepts that must be mastered to do well on the exam. We will focus on exactly how the Virginia EOC exam tests your biology skills, so you will know what to expect on exam day.

Lesson 1 includes test-taking strategies and techniques that are useful for the EOC Biology exam and any other biology test you take. Lessons 2–13 review all the biology concepts listed in the Virginia Standards of Learning for Biology. The concepts in these lessons are the same ones that are tested by the EOC Biology exam.

The book also includes two complete practice tests with answer keys and explanations, so that you can assess your skills under exam conditions. After you've worked through this book, there will be no surprises when you take the actual EOC Biology exam.

WHAT DO THE SOL EXAMS MEAN FOR GRADUATION?

This is a big question, and you should be clear on this before you proceed to the finer points of how to ace this test.

Virginia high school students must pass six of twelve possible EOC exams in order to graduate and receive a Standard Diploma. But if you aren't satisfied with a standard diploma, there's also an Advanced Studies Diploma, which requires that you pass nine of the twelve EOC exams.

Students in Virginia must pass at least one EOC exam in science in order to earn a diploma. These include the Virginia EOC Earth Science, Biology, and Chemistry exams.

If you want more information about an Advanced Studies Diploma, speak to a guidance counselor, teacher, or adminstrator at your school.

FREQUENTLY ASKED QUESTIONS

- **What Does the Test Look Like?**

  The SOL Biology exam tests four major skill sets called "Reporting Categories." Each evaluates specific biology concepts and skills. Later in the book, we will review all the specific skills you'll need to successfully complete the test. If you want to peek at them now, you can check out the VDOE Web site at www.pen.k12.va.us.

  There are sixty multiple-choice questions on the SOL End of Course Biology exam. The questions break down according to Reporting Categories in the following way:

Reporting Categories	Number of Questions	Covered in this Book
Scientific Investigations	11	
Life at the Molecular and Cellular Level	14	
Life at the Systems and Organisms Level	14	
Interaction of Life-Forms	11	
Total Number of Scored Questions:	**50**	
Field Test Items:	**10**	
Total Number of Questions:	**60**	

- **What is a Field Test Item?**

  A field test item is an experimental question that does not count toward your final score. Because you have no way of knowing which questions are field test items and which ones count toward your score, answer every question as if it counts toward your score. The test writers use students' performance on field test items to determine whether they've written good questions for use on future exams.

- **What is a Passing Score?**

  You have to answer correctly twenty-six out of the fifty scored questions to pass the EOC Biology exam. There are sixty total questions on the exam, but ten of them are field test items that do not count toward your score. These ten questions are mixed in with the fifty scored questions, so you won't be able to tell which questions really count as you take the test. Do yourself a favor and answer *all* the questions as if they count toward your final score.

LESSON 1
STRATEGIES AND TECHNIQUES

WHAT'S ON THE EOC BIOLOGY EXAM?

As if the PSATs and SATs don't create enough test anxiety, now you've got to pass a standardized final exam in biology in order to graduate! Relax, you've already taken an important first step—you've decided to prepare, and this book is going to help you score your best.

In this lesson, you will learn exactly which biology concepts are tested and how exam writers put their questions together. Believe it or not, there is a method to all this standardized testing madness, and understanding how exam items are constructed can sometimes help you solve problems. You will also gain some insight into the structure and format of the exam as well as an explanation of the scoring process. The strategies and techniques described over the next few pages will be critical in maximizing your score on this exam. For that reason, it's important that you not only understand these strategies and techniques but that you *use* them as well. We've been studying and constructing standardized tests for a long time and have the experience and knowledge necessary to make sure you're using your time wisely as you work through this book. That's just about enough talk; let's see some action.

THE RULES OF THE GAME

In some ways, it is helpful to think of a standardized test like the EOC in Biology as a game. Just like any game, this exam has to play by certain rules. These rules can become as significant a component of the test as the actual knowledge and skills that it is designed to test. Imagine that the tallest, strongest, fastest, and most agile high school athlete in the world has just joined your football team. When the ball is kicked to him, he stops the ball with his foot, and then kicks the ball toward a teammate. Unfortunately, a member of the other team picks up the ball and runs it in for a touchdown. Your team loses the game and is done for the season. Did your star player lack the skills he needed to perform well? Nope. He was a finely tuned athlete. What he did lack was an understanding of the rules of the game. In the same way, not understanding the rules of the EOC Biology exam can cost you just as dearly.

In a situation similar to the football player, two equally skilled biology students could end up with very different scores if one student knew the rules of the test and the other student didn't. Imagine that two equally skilled students, Leanne and Joe, were taking the EOC Biology exam. Both students knew the answers to twenty-five of the fifty questions. As it stands at this moment, both students would fail the exam. However, Leanne knew that there was no guessing penalty and therefore guessed on the remaining twenty-five questions. Joe didn't know the rule about guessing and left the remaining twenty-five questions blank. When the exams were scored, Leanne's guessing paid off with a **passing grade.** As it turns out, she correctly answered thirty-one out of fifty questions—the twenty-five she knew and six that she guessed right. Joe, who left twenty-five answers blank, went to summer school. Granted, this is an extreme case, but it does exemplify the importance of knowing the rules of the exam. So, here's a rundown of the rules, but don't worry, there aren't too many that you'll need to keep in mind as you take the EOCs.

THERE IS NO GUESSING PENALTY

Okay, this is getting a little redundant, but it's worth repeating. Unlike some of the other standardized tests, the EOC Biology exam does not penalize you for incorrect answers. **This means that regardless of how little you know about a question, never, never, never leave the answer to a question blank on your answer sheet.**

THE TEST IS UNTIMED

Before you turn in the exam and the answer sheet, review each question carefully and double-check your answers. It is not uncommon to accidentally bubble in the wrong circle. For example, suppose you know that **C** is the correct answer to a chosen question. Make sure that **C** is actually the answer that you bubbled in on the answer sheet. Also, take the time to reexamine questions that you had difficulty with. Sometimes returning to a question after working on other questions can help you see the one you had difficulty with in a whole new light. The bottom line is that you have as much time as you need—use it!

You can measure things and use a calculator

In general, most high school biology courses aren't math intensive. There won't be a huge number of problems that will require you to use these tools, but there will be occasions when you'll need them. You will be allowed to use a ruler (standard and metric) and a calculator on the exam.

STRATEGY

Here are a few more strategies that you may find helpful as you seek a passing grade on the EOC Biology exam.

MULTIPLE-CHOICE FORMAT: FRIEND AND POE

The most important thing that you can bring to the EOC Biology exam is a sound knowledge and functional understanding of the biology concepts that you have been studying in class all year long. In Lessons 2 through 13, you will review several key biology concepts.

The multiple choice questions on the EOC Biology exam are specifically designed to test your skills and understanding of fundamental concepts in biology. Unlike many problems in mathematics that require you to solve a problem using multiple steps, most questions in the EOC Biology exam can be tackled head-on.

The multiple-choice format lends itself to a few different strategies that are particularly helpful if you are unsure of an answer. First, it's important to point out the obvious. For every question that has a multiple-choice answer, the correct answer is right in front of you! However, there will always be questions for which the answers aren't so obvious. Often, you can answer these questions by using a handy little tool that is called POE, Process of Elimination.

Where to start

There are several terrific ways to help you prepare for this exam. At the top of the list is studying. Not the "all-nighter" type studying but good old-fashioned "let's do a little review every day" kind of studying. While you're studying, don't forget to review your laboratory investigations as well.

Learning to deal

On the day of the exam, you can start racking up points right away by reading through the questions first. Read *each word* of each question carefully. Missing one word in a question can change the meaning of the question or the "best answer" choice dramatically. Again, make sure that you bubble in your answer choice in the correct spot. Also, you should bubble *lightly* at first. If you press very hard when you first bubble in and need to change the answer later, the machine that grades the test might score the answer that you did not intend. A good rule to follow is *bubble in light to start,* **then lock your answers in by bubbling in dark.**

It is a good idea to go through the test and answer the less difficult questions first. Then, do a second pass through the exam and start spending time on those questions that you weren't sure of initially. Here's where test-taking strategies come in handy.

OUR FRIEND POE: THE PROCESS OF ELIMINATION

Explore the essence of POE using the following few examples:

Example 1   One function of the human endoskeleton is to—
   A   transmit impulses
   B   produce blood cells
   C   produce lactic acid
   D   store nitrogenous wastes

Do you feel like you could make a guess here? If not, take a closer look and start trimming the number of answers that you have to choose from. You can rule out **A** and **D** fairly quickly because you know that the *nervous system* transmits electrical impulses, not the skeletal system, and that nitrogenous wastes are stored in the bladder, an organ that is part of the *excretory system*, not the skeletal system. That leaves you with the proverbial 50/50 split. For some, it may be pure guesswork at this point. Even so, your odds of getting a question right are better when you're choosing between two answers—this gives you a 50 percent chance of getting a question right—than when you're choosing between four answers, which only gives you a 25 percent chance of hitting on the money. For the athletes in the crowd, it may dawn on them that their *muscles* produce lactic acid, causing stiffness and soreness. With all other possibilities eliminated, that leaves **B** as the correct answer.

A PICTURE IS WORTH A THOUSAND WORDS

Of course, there are going to be those test questions that really throw you for a loop—at first. Questions that have pictures with them don't have to give you trouble if you learn to "read the picture."

Example 2   The diagram below shows the same type of molecules in area *A* and area *B*. With the passage of time, some molecules move from area *A* to area *B*. This movement is the result of the process of—

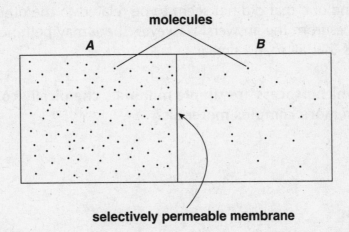

molecules

A   *B*

selectively permeable membrane

Learning to "read the picture" means that before you look at the answers, you should study the diagram carefully. As a matter of fact, cover the answers with your hand, so that you can focus more clearly on the picture. As you study the picture, describe it to yourself. For this example, you've already been told quite a bit of information about what's going on in the picture. The question asks you to identify the *process* that causes the molecules to move from area *A* to area *B*. Try to describe what's going on using appropriate terms for the *process* that is shown above. After you think that you've figured out the process and described how and why this process works for the question asked, uncover the answers to see if your process is among the answer choices.

    F phagocytosis

    G pinocytosis

    H diffusion

    J cyclosis

At this point, the best scenario is that when you uncovered your answers, you were delighted to find that **H**, diffusion, matched the process that you identified in the diagram above. If you guessed that the process that caused the movement was osmosis, you may have had a moment of panic when that answer choice wasn't among the actual choices. At this point, you could have realized that osmosis and diffusion are similar processes, and therefore, the answer must be **H**. If, however, you were left without a clue in the answer department, then you could have played the old Sesame Street "three of these things belong together, three of these things are kind of the same" game. Because three of the answers end in *-osis* and one does not, diffusion would be your best possible guess. This is often a good method to use as a last resort.

WHAT'S IN A NAME?

This brings you to the third point in discussing strategies for dealing with the EOC Biology exam. In the previous example, you were faced with three answers that sounded similar and one that did not seem to be related to the others at all. You gleaned lots of clues from the answers. However, there may be times when you are faced with choices that all sound similar.

Example 3 **In which process are simple materials chemically combined to form more complex materials?**

A Cyclosis

B Synthesis

C Hydrolysis

D Pinocytosis

Now, this could really be a tough one to crack. All the answers end in -*sis*. No help there. Therefore, see if the question can give you a better clue about how to look at the answers. If you go back to the question and put it into your own words, you can see that they want you to *chemically* combine simple stuff to make more complex stuff. So, the question seems to be about some sort of chemical reaction. Based on that information, you can throw out **A** and **D** because each of these processes is cellular. This leaves you with **B** and **C**. Well, the question itself and POE helped you reduce your answer options to two. At this point, you could "punt" and choose one of the answers based on your gut reaction, or you could try a little word association exercise. Remember that you've got all the time you need. Use it to get the best score that you can possibly get.

Word association helps you figure out a word meaning through association with other words that sound similar. For instance, the meaning of "hydrolysis" may not exactly leap out at you. Start to put together a list of words or phrases that sound similar, such as hydraulic, hydroelectric power, hydrologic cycle, and hydroencephalitis (okay, maybe not that one). In any event, after a while it may dawn on you that all the words containing *hydro-* have something to do with water. Let's do the same exercise for "synthesis." There's synthetic, which means man-made, and synthesizer, equipment used to put together music. Hmmm, it looks like a pretty strong case can be made for **B**, and that's your best bet.

Finally, a question is going to come along that absolutely defies all your tactics. This is biology after all, an age-old science built on lots and lots of vocabulary. Two study strategies that might come in handy for learning the nuts and bolts (aka vocabulary and concepts) of biology are flash cards and mnemonics. Do yourself a huge favor and make up individual flash cards for each topic. This is a time-tested way to get the vocabulary down that will get you through the really tough questions on the exam. Mnemonics are handy little word games that will help you remember specific information. For example, the commonly accepted taxonomic levels from largest and most general to smallest and most specific are **K**ingdom, **P**hylum, **C**lass, **O**rder, **F**amily, **G**enus, and **S**pecies. The following is a common mnemonic device used to remember the order and names of these taxonomic levels:

King **P**hilip **C**ame **O**ver **F**or **G**ood **S**oup.

WHAT DOES IT LOOK LIKE: IS THIS ON THE TEST?

The Virginia School Board is very specific about the topics they expect you to know for the SOL Biology exam. In fact, the SOL Biology exam have been broken down into four major reporting categories. You will explore the details of each reporting category in detail in the chapters that follow.

The test itself is sixty questions long. Of the sixty questions, fifty will count toward your final score. Because there is no way to know which ten questions are experimental, you need to treat each and every question on the exam as the real thing because for all intents and purposes, it is. With that in mind, each reporting category is represented by a specific number of exam items designed to test your knowledge and skills as they relate to specific **Standards of Learning.** A chart representing the breakdown of questions on the SOL Biology exam can be found on page 3.

Wait, what's a field test item anyway? A field test item is a question that the exam writers have written but are a bit unsure about. Field test items are included on actual EOC exams to determine how good these questions are and whether they should be included on future exams.

It's important to note that unlike traditional standardized tests such as the PSAT and SAT, the EOC in Biology *does not* proceed along a significant order of increasing difficulty. In other words, the EOC in Biology doesn't get harder as you move through the exam from beginning to end.

By now you know that the EOC in Biology is a multiple-choice exam that consists of sixty questions, and although you are required to answer all sixty questions, your actual score will be the number of correct answers you got on fifty particular questions. You also know that you need to get twenty-six out of fifty questions right in order to be proficient, and that forty-five right answers out of a possible fifty earns you an Advanced Proficiency mark. What you may or may not know after looking at the examples provided earlier in this lesson is the format of the individual questions.

The answer choices for odd-numbered questions (1, 3, 5, and so on) will be indicated by the letters **A, B, C,** and **D.** Answer choices for even-numbered questions (2, 4, 6, and so on) will be indicated by the letters **F, G, H** and **J.**

HOW IS THE BIOLOGY EXAM SCORED?

As indicated earlier, a machine will score your answer sheet along with those of every biology student in Virginia. A "test corrector person" will run an answer key containing all the right answers through the machine first, followed by student answer sheets. The machine automatically records your score on your answer sheet. Because a machine does the scoring, it's important that you do everything in your power to help the machine pick up the answer that you had intended. Remember to bubble in light at first, just in case you want to go back and change the answers to some of your questions. If you initially bubble in dark and have to erase an answer, the machine may pick up the answer that was not your final answer. Final scores are usually released about six weeks after you took the exam. Seniors receive priority.

WRAPPING IT UP

Our final tips are going to sound a bit cheesy, but we're going to share them anyway. Prepare for the exam well in advance of test day, eat well, sleep well, and then show your best stuff.

LESSON 2
SCIENTIFIC INVESTIGATIONS

DO I REALLY NEED TO KNOW THAT?

The answer is yes. The SOL Biology exam not only tests your knowledge of biological concepts and theories, but also your grasp of the scientific process in general. This process is better known as the "scientific method," and the Virginia Department of Education is *very* interested in having you know it. You've probably seen and used the scientific method in most of your lab classes, but just to refresh your memory, here's a rundown of what it is.

- Observations of living things are recorded in the lab and in the field.
- Hypotheses are formulated based on observations.
- Variables are defined and investigations are designed to test hypotheses.
- Graphing and arithmetic calculations are used as tools in data analysis.
- Conclusions are formed based on recorded quantitative and qualitative data.
- Impacts of sources of error inherent in experimental design are identified and discussed.
- Validity of data is determined.
- Alternative explanations and models are recognized and analyzed.
- Appropriate technology is used for gathering and analyzing data and communicating results.
- Research is used, based on popular and scientific literature.

The scientific method is a generic phrase applied to a system of problem-solving steps and skills. It's not a single way of approaching questions in science, but it *does* provide some general guidelines for investigating problems and determining their answers. The scientific method is all about using critical thinking, technical, and research skills to identify and investigate problems.

If the list above seems a little intimidating, don't worry. Here is the simplified version of the scientific method: make observations, formulate a question based on those observations, formulate a hypothesis, develop an experiment to test the hypothesis, gather data, analyze data, record results of data analysis, and draw a conclusion based on data. If the results support the hypothesis, then it may be necessary to repeat the experiment to demonstrate the reproducibility of the results. Reproducibility is just one method for validating not so much what the results indicate, but rather the appropriateness of experimental design for the question under investigation and the reliability of the results themselves.

The absolute first step in the scientific method involves **observation.** Observation is the act of gathering information about a system or environment using one or more of your five senses. Observation should not be confused with **inference,** which is a conclusion based on observations and scientific knowledge. Observations provide the information needed to formulate a question. For example, biologists monitoring a population of big-eared bats may make the observation that the population size is declining. Based on their observations, the biologists formulate the question: **Why is the population of big-eared bats declining?**

A **hypothesis** is an "educated guess" or prediction about the answer to the question, or solution to the problem. Hypotheses are often phrased as statements and are formulated by taking into account all the known information about a situation. You can try to make a hypothesis about the population decline of the bats, taking their biology into account. Suppose that the population of feral house cats (domestic cats that live outdoors all year long) is increasing in the area. Because these cats are known predators of big-eared bats, it might be that the bat population is decreasing due to increased predation pressure by the feral house cats. This is now your hypothesis.

> **TIP:** Statistical analysis really just means that the data (i.e., numbers) you've gathered will be analyzed in search of a trend or pattern.

Once you have a hypothesis in place, the next steps are to identify the **variables** that affect the system, and to use these variables to design an appropriate test to validate or disprove the hypothesis. Variables are factors that change and can be measured in the experiment. Ideally, in a well-designed experiment, only a single variable changes, while all others remain constant. The experiment would therefore test the impact of one variable on a system. A **control** is a standard against which experimental results can be measured. Every well-designed experiment has a control or standard used for comparison. As you design your experiment to test the hypothesis that feral cats (our variable in this experiment) are causing a decline in bat populations, you need to locate big-eared bat populations in locations that have little or no contact with feral cats. This population would act as a control against which you can compare the results of your studies of other bat populations exposed to feral cat populations.

When designing an experiment to test a hypothesis, the technology with which you will gather data must be appropriate for your task. Bats are nocturnal mammals that roost during the day in caves. Initially, the most appropriate technology for this type of investigation may include flashlights and hard hats. Data gathered through weekly counts of both bat and cat populations for the duration of several months can then be inputted into a computer program that performs statistical analysis.

Many statistical programs generate graphs that are useful analytical tools that diagram the interrelationships between variables. In this case, the populations of bats and cats from different areas would be the variables.

A LITTLE GRAPHING 101

Line graphs are pictorial representations of the relationships between variables. Each graph consists of a **vertical axis** that intersects a **horizontal axis** at the **origin.** The **independent variable,** the variable that the biologist has no control over, is recorded on the horizontal or *x*-axis. The **dependent variable,** the variable that changes because of the independent variable, is recorded on the vertical or *y*-axis. In general, there are four types of relationships that can be illustrated on a line graph: direct, inverse, constant, and cyclical.

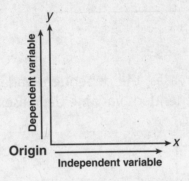

Direct relationship

As the independent variable increases, the dependent variable also *increases*.

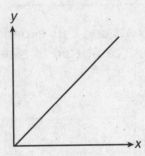

Inverse relationship

As the independent variable increases, the dependent variable *decreases*.

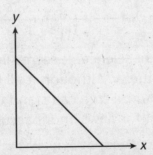

Constant relationship

As the independent variable increases, the dependent variable remains the same.

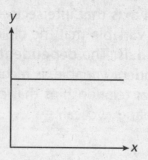

Cyclical relationship

As the independent variable increases, the dependent variable also increases up to a certain point, after which the dependent variable decreases.

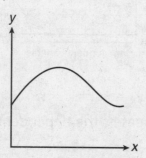

How does this fit into the earlier bats and cats experiment? After counting the bats and cats over a period of time, one can begin to assemble and analyze the data to determine if their hypothesis is correct.

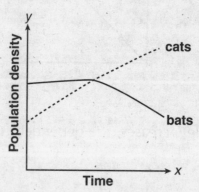

Now comes the interesting part of science. It seems from the graph above that the data collected support the hypothesis. Although it all looks good, one would have to make sure that what appears to be true can stand up to scrutiny. You should be able to examine your experiment for flaws and inaccuracies that may have been caused by the lack of precision of your instruments, poorly designed or inadequate experimental controls, human error, or any number of other related factors that would cause the data to be incorrect.

What if your results and conclusions do not support the hypothesis? Then, it's pretty much back to the drawing board. If the data indicate that bat populations decline at similar rates no matter what the density of feral cats, then it's fairly safe to say that cats are not impacting bat populations. You would then need to return to the initial question again, why the bat populations are declining, and formulate a new hypothesis based on other variables.

When formulating a question or hypothesis, you shouldn't underestimate the value of research using primary and secondary literature sources as you develop a research project of your own. Primary literature sources include professional journals such as *Science* and *Proceedings from the National Academy of Science*. Virtually every field within the life sciences has its own professional journal in which scientists publish information about their research investigations, including experimental design, results, and conclusions. These are great sources of information and should be used whenever possible. On the other hand, because professional scientists write these articles, they can get a little hairy in terms of technical information. *Scientific American* and *Discover* are two good secondary sources. Secondary science literature is composed of science articles that are geared to provide much of the same information as the primary sources, but without the nitty-gritty detail of experimental design and tons of jargon that may be difficult for the average non-researcher to grasp.

A final word about data and conclusions: Although the data may *appear* to support the hypotheses, it is very important for researchers to explore other options that may also provide explanations for observations. In our hypothetical study of bats and cats, bat populations did appear to decrease as cat populations increased. However, because cats are not generally adapted to a wild existence, you might infer that large cat populations are the result of large human populations. Research has indicated that human disturbances of bat roost sites and maternity caves have negatively impacted big-eared bat populations. So, the next step in validating the data of the original study may be to rule out human impact on population mortality.

Now that you have a basic understanding of the tools used to conduct a scientific study, it's time to move on and review the general understanding of the biological world that most scientists share.

Remember, this book is only meant to be a *review* of biological concepts. It is not meant to replace your textbook. Keep your biology textbook handy to help you learn the in-depth details of biology. If you don't feel that you have a handle on what you're reviewing, just go back to your textbook and refresh your memory.

REVIEW FOR LESSONS 1 AND 2

Take a few moments to practice test-taking strategies for questions about the scientific method and experimental design. The answers and explanations are on page 21.

1 A student notices that a water plant placed in bright light gives off bubbles. The student wants to design an experiment to investigate the effect of light intensity on the rate of bubble production. What would be an appropriate experimental design to test the effect of light intensity on the rate of bubble production?

A Place one plant at a fixed distance from the light source while varying the distance of another plant from the same light source.

B Place two plants the same distance from the same light source.

C Place two plants at a fixed distance from different light sources; expose one plant to white light and the other to blue light.

D Place one plant in water containing a high concentration of oxygen and another plant in water containing a high concentration of carbon dioxide.

2 A laboratory investigation is set up to determine if the hormone thyroxin increases metabolic activity in rats. Twenty rats of the same species, age, and weight are selected and divided into two equal groups. All other factors in the investigation are kept the same, except that one group is given distilled water, while the other group is given distilled water containing thyroxin.

The variable being studied in this experiment is the—

F effect of age on growth

G effect of weight on growth

H effect of thyroxin on growth

J effect of species on growth

3 One ounce each of protein, fat, and carbohydrate and are burned separately in a calorimeter to determine caloric content. The results are shown in the data table below.

Organic compound	Number of calories produced
Protein	147
Fat	271
Carbohydrate	152

Which statement represents a valid conclusion based on the data?

A An ounce of fat contains almost twice as many calories as an ounce of protein.

B An ounce of protein burns more efficiently than an ounce of carbohydrate.

C An ounce of carbohydrate produces the same number of calories as an ounce of protein.

D Proteins and carbohydrates provide the most calories per ounce.

4 An investigation was designed to determine the effect of ultraviolet light on mold spore growth. Two groups of mold spores were grown under identical conditions, except that one group was exposed to ultraviolet light, while the other group was grown in total darkness. In this investigation, the group of mold spores grown without any ultrviolet light is known as the—

F hypothesis

G control

H limiting factor

J experimental variable

ANSWERS AND EXPLANATIONS

1 **A Place one plant at a fixed distance from the light source while varying the distance of another plant from the same light source.** This selection has both a control, a plant at a fixed location, and a variable, changing the distance of a plant from the light source. **B** lacks a variable. **C** tests the effect the wavelengths of the light received at the same distance. **D** does not work at all for this particular question.

2 **H effect of thyroxin on growth. F, G,** and **J** are variables that do not change.

3 **A An ounce of fat contains almost twice as many calories as an ounce of protein.**

4 **G control. J,** ultraviolet light, is the experimental variable. **F** and **H** do not apply.

LESSON 3
LIFE AT THE MOLECULAR LEVEL

WATER: THE UNDERRATED MOLECULE

Water is perhaps one of the most underappreciated molecules on Earth. More than 60 percent of the human body is made of water. Additionally, water covers more than 70 percent of Earth's surface and is the only substance on Earth that occurs naturally in all three

TIP: Covalent bonding means that the oxygen atom is sharing a pair of negatively charged electrons particles with each hydrogen atom.

phases: solid, liquid, and gas. What makes this molecule particularly nifty is not so much its existence, but rather how its unique physical and chemical structure allows life to exist.

Your ordinary, run-of-the-mill water molecule is made of two hydrogen atoms **covalently** bonded to one oxygen atom.

Here's where it gets interesting. Because the oxygen atom is a bit bigger and has a bit stronger positive charge in its nucleus than the hydrogen atom, the oxygen atom doesn't share the electrons equally with the hydrogen atoms. This unequal sharing causes one side of the water molecule to have a slightly negative charge, and the other to have a slightly positive charge. This creates an electrically **polar** structure. The attraction between the positive end of one water molecule and the negative end of another water molecule causes the formation of a **hydrogen bond.** Hydrogen bonds are weak bonds that link polar molecules together. It is these bonds that lead to the following unique properties of water:

- Have you ever been to the beach just as the weather is turning cold? If you have, you've probably noticed that the water feels warmer than the air around you, even though it is the middle of the fall. Why does ocean water stay warm much longer than you think it would? Well, water has a **high specific heat.** That means that it takes a lot of energy to increase its temperature. It takes all summer and the blazing Sun to increase the ocean's temperature by just a few degrees. Water's ability to resist temperature change is one of the factors that help keep the temperature in our oceans fairly stable. It's also why humans are able to keep a normal constant body temperature of 98.6 degrees fahrenheit.

- In most living systems, water's polarity causes it to act as a "universal solvent"—it can dissolve many kinds of substances. After these substances have been dissolved, they can be more easily transported throughout an organism.

- Water molecules have a strong tendency to stick together. This property is called **cohesion.** For example, when water molecules evaporate from a leaf, they "tug" neighboring molecules. These, in turn, draw up the molecules immediately behind them, and so on, all the way down the plant vessels. The resulting chain of water molecules enables water to move up the stem.

- Water molecules also like to stick to *other* substances—that is, they're **adhesive.** (Remember in lab class, when you tried to take apart two glass slides stuck together by a film of water?). The combination of cohesion and adhesion accounts for the ability of water to rise tens of hundreds of feet up the roots, trunks, and branches of the largest trees. Because this phenomenon occurs in plants' thin vessels, it is called **capillary action.**

Here's a little recap before moving on.

- Water is polar and serves as a universal solvent for many other substances.
- Water has a high specific heat.
- Water has cohesive and adhesive properties, allowing for capillary action to take place in trees.

THE FAB FOUR: THE STRUCTURE AND FUNCTION OF MACROMOLECULES

Although living things come in all shapes and sizes, they are all made of the same four basic kinds of substances, called **macromolecules.** The macromolecules include carbohydrates, lipids, proteins, and nucleic acids.

CARBOHYDRATES

Carbohydrates are **organic**—contain the element carbon—compounds composed of carbon, hydrogen, and oxygen atoms. Similar to other organic compounds, carbon atoms bond together, forming a "skeleton" around which hydrogen and oxygen atoms are distributed.

The general formula of carbohydrates is represented by $(CH_2O)n$, where n is equal to the number of carbon atoms in the carbohydrate molecule. The remaining hydrogen and oxygen atoms associated with a carbohydrate molecule are generally found in the proportion 2:1.

Ring form of glucose

Straight-chain form of glucose

Ring form of fructose

Straight-chain form of fructose

Carbohydrates play a key role in both producing and storing energy throughout the body of an organism. Carbohydrates are separated into three different categories—**monosaccharides, disaccharides,** and **polysaccharides.** Monosaccharides are carbohydrates in their simplest form. In other words, these simple sugars cannot be broken down into smaller carbohydrate molecules. Glucose is the most abundant monosaccharide, as it is found in virtually all living things. It consists of just six carbon atoms, in addition to hydrogen and oxygen.

Before going any further, take a moment to familiarize yourself with a little memory tool. If it all seems Greek to you, that's okay, because it is.

- *Mono-* means "one."
- *Di-* means "two."
- *Poly-* means "many."
- *-saccharide* means "sugar."

Okay, so what do you get when you add one monosaccharide to another monosaccharide? A **disaccharide**—a carbohydrate formed through **dehydration synthesis.** Some common disaccharides are sucrose, lactose, and maltose.

> **TIP:** What if you don't remember how dehydration synthesis works? Piece of cake. Just break the word apart. *Dehydration* refers to the removal of water. *Synthesis* means the manufacturing of a new molecule. So, if you have two monosaccharides, you get a disaccharide by combining them and removing a water molecule in the process. Finally, something easy to remember.

Remember our old friend, the hydrogen bond? Well, the hydrogen bonds that form between carbohydrate molecules result in the formation of bigger and more complex carbohydrate molecules called **polysaccharides.** Whereas monosaccharides like glucose act as energy sources, polysaccharides, such as starch and glycogen, are storage forms of carbohydrates. Polysaccharides also provide structural material for some organisms, such as **cellulose** in plants.

Remember: Plants use **starch** to store glucose. Animals use **glycogen** to store glucose.

LIPIDS

Lipids are a large group of organic macromolecules that are all insoluble—do not dissolve—in water. This is where your fats, oils, steroids, waxes, and related compounds come into play. Just like a carbohydrate molecule, a lipid molecule starts out as a chain of carbon atoms bonded together with hydrogen and oxygen atoms. However, the proportion of the hydrogen to oxygen atoms is *not* 2:1. As a matter of fact, there is no uniform ratio of hydrogen to oxygen atoms in lipid molecules. Instead, lipids contain three *fatty acids* and one *glycerol* molecule (an alcohol with three carbons).

The carbon and hydrogen atoms are usually bonded to an **alcohol** group (-OH) or an acid—also called a **carboxyl**—group (-COOH).

The most common type of fats are **triglycerides, saturated fats,** and **unsaturated fats.** Triglycerides are composed of four molecules of glycerol and three fatty acids. Each triglyceride is different depending on the types of fatty acids that bond to each glycerol molecule. Just remember, when you see the word triglycerides, it's just a fancy-schmancy way of saying fat.

Everybody talks about saturated and unsaturated fat. But do you know what they mean? A saturated fat contains only single bonds between carbons. It's usually solid and produced only by animals. Beef fat (like in a hamburger) and butter are examples of saturated fat. An unsaturated fat contains at least one double bond between the carbon atoms. You usually find unsaturated fat in the form of a liquid, such as corn oil and olive oil.

Other lipids include waxes, which are long chains of fatty acids bonded to alcohol. Lipids with ringlike structures are called steroids. These are usually pigments in plants or hormones in animals. Chlorophyll, estrogen, and cortisone are all examples of steroids.

PROTEINS

Proteins are the most abundant macromolecules found in living things. Proteins are the key structural elements in almost all living things, including cell membranes, skin, muscle, blood, feathers, fins, and fur. In addition to their structural functions, special proteins called **enzymes** serve important biochemical functions, as they assist chemical reactions that take place inside the cells of organisms.

Similar to carbohydrates and lipids, proteins are composed of carbon, hydrogen, and oxygen. The presence of nitrogen sets proteins apart from these other macromolecules. Proteins are made up of repeating **amino acid** units. Twenty different amino acids function as the building blocks of all proteins in living things. All amino acids boil down to the same basic structure. Amino acids contain an **amine** group ($-NH_2$) and a **carboxyl** group (-COOH) attached to a central carbon atom. So, how do you tell the amino acids apart? In addition to the amine and carboxyl groups, each amino acid has a third molecular group attached to the central carbon atom. The third group, **radical (R),** is different for each amino acid. These R-groups determine the physical and chemical characteristics of each amino acid and, therefore, determine how the proteins that they comprise are formed.

Joining two amino acid groups together through dehydration synthesis forms a **dipeptide.** There's that prefix again. If three or more amino acids are chemically bonded together through dehydration synthesis, what kind of molecule is produced? If you guessed that a **polypeptide** is produced, you're right on the money. If *two* amino acids produce a *di*peptide, then *three* or more amino acids will produce a *poly*peptide. Proteins are composed of one or more polypeptides.

NUCLEIC ACIDS

The fourth group of macromolecules, nucleic acids, is made up of repeating units called **nucleotides.** Each nucleotide is made up of a five-carbon sugar with an attached phosphate (PO_4-) group. A nitrogenous base is also attached to the five-carbon sugar. Each nitrogenous base is made up of, you guessed it, carbon, hydrogen, oxygen, and of course, nitrogen.

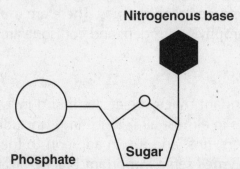

Chemically bonding nucleotides together produces a chain of nucleotides called a **nucleic acid.** There are two types of nucleic acids found in cells: **deoxribonucleic acid (DNA)** and **ribonucleic acid (RNA). DNA** is important because it stores genetic information. **RNA** is essential for protein synthesis. You will learn more about DNA and RNA later.

THE NATURE OF ENZYMES

As you read earlier, proteins are a class of macromolecules commonly found in living systems. A special group of proteins, called enzymes, plays a functional role in the chemical reactions that take place inside cells. In fact, many cellular chemical reactions wouldn't take place if it were not for enzymes. There are a few critical points that you will need to remember about these molecules.

WHAT DO ENZYMES DO?

To better understand what enzymes do, it's important to get a handle on what's going on during chemical reactions. In the simplest terms, a chemical reaction is the result of the chemical interaction between *reactants* that results in the formation of *products.*

$$\text{Reactant + Reactant} \longrightarrow \text{Products}$$

Chemical reactions take place when chemical bonds are either formed or broken. Several conditions must be present for chemical reactions to take place. First and foremost, the reactants must come into contact with each other. The second critical component necessary for a chemical reaction to take place is energy. **Activation energy** is the energy needed for a reaction to start.

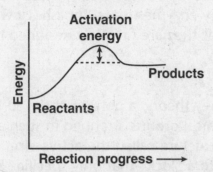

In this type of system, reactants wander around with some of the reactants, eventually colliding with enough energy for products to form. Unfortunately, biological systems do not have the luxury of simply waiting around for the right reactions to happen at the right time. That's where enzymes come in.

Enzymes act as **catalysts,** molecules that, when added to a chemical reaction, will speed up the rate at which products are formed by lowering the activation energy required for the reaction to start.

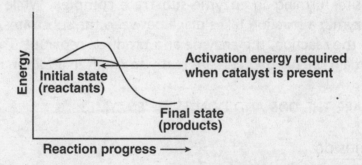

Catalysts regulate the reaction rate in a chemical system. Although the catalyst mediates the chemical reaction, the catalyst itself remains unchanged. Keep in mind that in an enzyme-aided reaction, reactants are referred to as **substrates.**

SO, HOW DO ENZYMES WORK?

Most enzymes have very specific job descriptions. For example, amylase is an enzyme whose sole purpose is catalyzing the breakdown of the polysaccharide, starch, to the monosaccharide, glucose. There are thousands of enzymes and substrate molecules in a living system. Finding the right substrates to match the right enzymes would seem a daunting task for any enzyme to accomplish. However, enzymes hold the key to finding the substrates that they are uniquely designed to accommodate.

LOCK-AND-KEY THEORY

According to the lock-and-key theory, a portion of the surface of each enzyme is made up of a series of chemical groups arranged in such a way that they form a three-dimensional surface structure called the **active site.** The active site is believed to operate in a way similar to a "lock" that only specific "keys" (substrates) will fit.

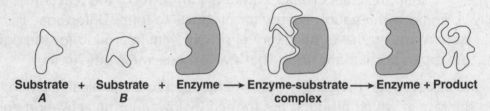

Substrate + Substrate + Enzyme ⟶ Enzyme-substrate ⟶ Enzyme + Product
A   B   complex

Once an enzyme finds the correct substrate, the substrate is bound to the enzyme's active site, forming an **enzyme-substrate complex**. While bound to the surface of the enzyme, a reaction takes place between the substrates, forming products. At the end of the reaction, the enzyme and products separate. The enzyme and its active site remain unchanged and are ready to catalyze additional reactions.

HERE ARE THE DOS AND DON'TS OF ENZYMES

Enzymes do
- increase the rate of a reaction by lowering the reaction's activation energy
- form temporary enzyme-substrate complexes
- remain unaffected by the reaction

Enzymes don't
- change in the reaction
- make reactions occur that would otherwise not occur

WHAT CONTROLS ENZYME ACTIVITY AND REACTION RATE?

How well enzymes perform their designated roles is determined by several variables.

1. **Concentration:** the rate of enzyme-regulated reactions can be increased by increasing the number (concentration) of substrate molecules available to the reactions. However, at some point, usually when the concentration of substrates is equal to the concentration of enzyme, the reaction rate can no longer be increased through the addition of more substrate molecules.

2. **Temperature:** each enzyme operates within a specific optimal temperature range. When temperatures are not optimal, enzymatic reactions decrease. Extreme temperature variation can cause enzyme activity, and therefore chemical reactions, to stop altogether.

3. **Cell acidity:** each enzyme operates best within a specific pH range. The **pH scale**, which ranges from 0 to 14, is used to represent the acidity or alkalinity of a solution. Acidity is a measure of the relative concentration of hydrogen ions (H+) in a solution. Solutions that have pH values less than 7 are acidic, and solutions that have pH values greater than 7 are alkaline. Solutions that have pH values of 7 are neither acidic nor alkaline. These solutions are neutral.

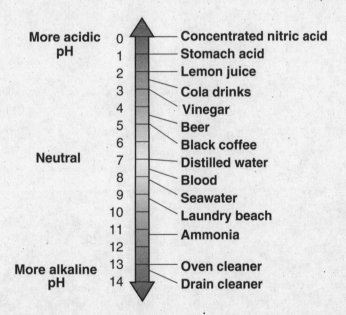

With a few exceptions, most tissues and fluids in the body of organisms have pH values in the neighborhood of 7. Therefore, many of the enzymes that operate in living systems function optimally in environments that have pH values around 7. Changes in pH, even minor ones, can significantly impact enzyme function, causing a decrease in reaction rate. Significant changes can, and often do, cause enzyme functions to shut down.

A quick word about coenzymes

Special organic molecules called **coenzymes** are found in low concentrations in organic systems, or are generated on an as-needed basis to assist enzymes in their catalytic functions. While coenzymes are organic, they are not proteins. Many vitamins function as coenzymes that assist cellular reactions.

REVIEW FOR LESSON 3

Take a few moments to practice the test-taking strategies for questions about chemistry. The answers and explanations are on page 34.

1 **Which inorganic substance found in living things aids in the diffusion of gases through a cell membrane?**

  A Water

  B Glucose

  C Protein

  D Salt

2 **Which element is present in amylase but *not* in amylose?**

  F Carbon

  G Hydrogen

  H Oxygen

  J Nitrogen

3 **Which polymer contains repeating units known as nucleotides?**

  A Protein

  B DNA

  C Starch

  D Oil

4 **An enzyme-substrate complex may result from the interaction of molecules of—**

  F glucose and protease

  G sucrose and maltase

  H fat and lipase

  J protein and amylase

5 **What is the role of vitamins such as niacin in enzyme-controlled reactions?**

  A Vitamins are carbohydrates.

  B Vitamins are proteins.

  C Vitamins are nucleotides.

  D Vitamins are coenzymes.

ANSWERS AND EXPLANATIONS

1 **A Water.** Hmm . . . the question is looking for an inorganic substance that helps move things into and out of the cell. Try using POE to eliminate some of the choices. You know that inorganic substances are substances that do not contain carbon and hydrogen. Both **B** and **C** can be ruled out because they are organic. That leaves water and salt. Both of these choices are inorganic. However, **D**, salt, is a mineral that may be dissolved in water. Remember, water serves as a universal solvent.

2 **H Protein.** The ending -*ose* signifies that amylose is a carbohydrate. Carbohydrates such as glucose consist of carbon, hydrogen, and oxygen. The ending -*ase* signifies that amylase is an enzyme. Enzymes are proteins. Proteins consist of carbon, hydrogen, oxygen, and *nitrogen*. Nitrogen is in the amine group that is part of the amino acids that make up each protein.

3 **B DNA.** What is this question really asking? When nucleotides are strung together, they make what? Nucleotides are molecules that consist of a sugar, phosphate, and nitrogenous base such as adenine or guanine. **A** is composed of amino acid subunits. **C** is composed of glucose subunits. **D** is composed of fatty acid subunits.

4 **H fat and lipase.** Lipases are a group of enzymes that act on lipids (fats). Enzymes are often named for the substrate on which they work. For example, amyl*ose* (substrate) and amyl*ase* (enzyme) form an enzyme-substrate complex, so **J** is incorrect. *Prote*ases act on *prot*eins, so **F** is incorrect. *Malt*ase acts on *malt*ose, so **G** is incorrect.

5 **D Vitamins are coenzymes.** What's the question really asking? What do vitamins do? Assist in enzyme-controlled reactions. **A** and **B** are nutrient macromolecules. **C** is not true.

LESSON 4
PHOTOSYNTHESIS AND CELLULAR RESPIRATION

In the previous lesson, you learned that nearly every activity the cell performs requires energy. So, where does this energy come from? In nature, living things can be divided into groups based on how they obtain the energy needed to satisfy their metabolic appetites. **Autotrophs,** or producers, are organisms that are able to make their own organic molecules (food) from inorganic sources. Plants and algae are examples of autotrophs. **Heterotrophs,** or consumers, need "ready-made" macromolecules to satisfy their energy requirements. Although autotrophs and heterotrophs obtain their food in very different ways, they both rely on the processes of **photosynthesis** and **cellular respiration** to create adenosine triphosphate (ATP), their primary energy source.

PHOTOSYNTHESIS

If you look at it, life as a plant isn't so bad. They don't have to run around hunting prey or wait in long drive-thru lines just to get a bite to eat. As producers, all they have to do is bask in the Sun and churn out the glucose necessary for life. But don't be mistaken; producing glucose is no picnic. It's a complicated process involving several steps. Have a look at this process called photosynthesis.

Photosynthesis is a series of biochemical reactions during which the reactants—sunlight (electromagnetic energy at the wavelengths of visible light), carbon dioxide (CO_2), and water (H_2O)—are used to generate glucose ($C_6H_{12}O_6$), water (H_2O), and molecular oxygen (O_2).

The following is an overview:

$$6CO_2 + 6H_2O + sunlight \rightarrow C_6H_{12}O_6 + O_2$$

LOCATION

So, where does all this take place? Well, each cell contains **organelles,** tiny compartments where specific processes take place, just like the rooms of a house. In green plants and algae, **chloroplasts** are the sites for the initial stage of photosynthesis. Inside chloroplasts are stacks of coinlike structures called **grana.** The granas' membranes contain specialized pigments called **chlorophylls** and **carotinoids,** which help catalyze the light reaction. Chlorophyll also gives plants their characteristic green color.

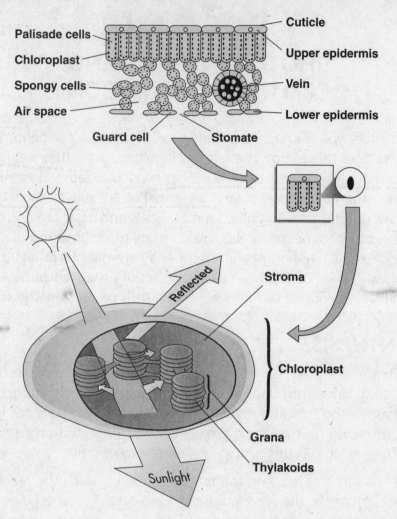

The two stages in photosynthesis are the light reaction and the dark reaction. These stages actually operate in series with the products from the light reaction becoming the reactants for the dark.

The Light Reaction

The light reaction starts when the photons (or energy units) of sunlight strike a leaf, activating chlorophyll and exciting electrons. The solar energy is then absorbed by the photosynthetic pigments and used to split a water molecule into its components—hydrogen and oxygen. The freed oxygen atoms are then able to bond and form the all-important atmospheric oxygen (O_2). The hydrogen atoms then bond to a carrier molecule to get them into the dark reaction. The carrier is called nicotinamide adenine dinucleotide phosphate (**NADP+**). The splitting of water molecules also produces electrons that get the energy ball rolling along the **electron transport chain.** The energy carried by these electrons are used to power the formation of ATP, the energy currency of cells. The whole point of the light reaction is to produce two things: energy in the form of ATP and hydrogen carriers, specifically NADP+.

THE DARK REACTION

The second stage of photosynthesis does not require the presence of sunlight and has therefore been coined the dark reaction, or the Calvin cycle (after its discoverer Melvin Calvin). The ATP and NADPH created during the light reaction combine with carbon dioxide and, through the magic of several enzymes, form glucose and other organic molecules. Glucose molecules then become the starting reactants used to power the processes involved in cellular respiration.

VARIABLES AFFECTING THE RATE OF PHOTOSYNTHESIS

Photosynthetic rate is directly affected by environmental variables including the following:
- light intensity
- carbon dioxide concentration
- temperature

Remember: The rate of enzyme catalyzed reactions can be increased by increasing the concentration of substrate molecules and that increasing the substrate concentration increases reaction rate until the concentration of substrate molecules is equal to the concentration of the enzyme. Photosynthesis relies heavily on a number of different enzymes to get the job done. Increasing the concentration of reactants involved in photosynthesis increases the reaction rate. Additionally, changing the temperature of the system affects the rate of photosynthesis.

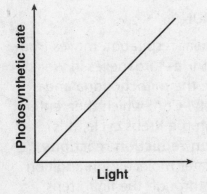
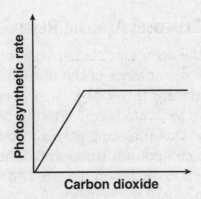
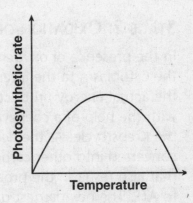

CELLULAR RESPIRATION

Both plants and animals must carry out respiration. Cellular respiration is a series of biochemical reactions during which the reactants produced during photosynthesis—carbohydrates and molecular oxygen—react to form carbon dioxide, water, and ATP. A simplified equation representing these reactions appears below.

$$C_6H_{12}O_6 + O_2 \rightarrow CO_2 + H_2O + 36 \text{ ATP}$$

TIP: Of course, when you're studying biology, memorizing terms is half the battle. So, just in case you forget the difference between aerobic and anaerobic, *remember* that after you do **a**erobics you might need some **a**ir (oxygen) to recuperate. It's simple, even cheesy perhaps, but it works!

Cellular respiration occurs in two different forms: **aerobic respiration** and **anaerobic respiration.** If oxygen is present, ATP is produced via aerobic respiration. If oxygen is not present, then cells rely on anaerobic respiration to generate their energy.

Here's a closer look at the necessary stages for cellular respiration.

STAGE 1: GLYCOLYSIS

Glycolysis is the first stage of cellular respiration and does *not* require oxygen. Therefore, it is considered an anaerobic process. During this stage, the glucose produced during photosynthesis is broken down to create **pyruvic acid**, which is found in the cytoplasm of cells. Here's the simplified equation.

Glucose + 2 ATP → 2 Pyruvic acid + 4 ATP

The following are two things to remember about glycolysis:
- It occurs in the cytoplasm.
- It is an *anaerobic* process.

STAGE 2: OXIDATION OF GLUCOSE: AEROBIC RESPIRATION

In the presence of oxygen, the action for stage two in cellular respiration moves from the cytoplasm to the interior membranes of the **mitochondria**—organelles in which the actual energy production steps take place. Once inside the mitochondria and with the help of a coenzyme, pyruvate is converted to acetyl-CoA, which then enters the Krebs cycle. As the acetyl-CoA molecule passes through the Krebs cycle, it is converted into other carbon compounds through **oxidation-reduction reactions** that also result in the production of carbon dioxide and water molecules in addition to ATP. The next largest gain of ATP molecules is acquired through the final steps of the aerobic respiration process that takes place in the electron transport chain in the inner membrane of mitochondria. Taken together, the process of *aerobic* cellular respiration results in the production of thirty-six ATP molecules, which become the energy source that fuels all other cellular activities.

AND WHAT ABOUT ANAEROBIC RESPIRATION?

When there is no oxygen present, cellular respiration processes must take place along a different path and result in a much less energetic outcome. Under **anaerobic** conditions, pyruvate molecules produced during glycolysis remain in the cytoplasm and undergo **fermentation** reactions. There are two types of fermentation reactions, each resulting in a net gain of just two ATP molecules that differ only in the secondary by-products produced. During the alcoholic fermentation that takes place in bacteria and certain fungi such as yeast, ethyl alcohol and CO_2 are produced in addition to ATP. Humans have learned to harness these products and employ them in the production of bread, cheese, yogurt, and alcoholic beverages. During lactic acid fermentation, lactic acid is produced in addition to ATP.

FUN FACT: Although humans are aerobic organisms by nature, human muscle cells can actually ferment. When you exercise, your muscles require a lot of energy. Your muscles need to convert huge amounts of glucose to ATP. But while you continue to exercise, your body might not get all the oxygen it needs. Your muscle cells then switch over to anaerobic respiration that converts pyruvic acid into lactic acid. This causes that oh-so uncomfortable muscle cramp. Maybe you can try telling this to your gym teacher to cut down on the number of laps you have to run.

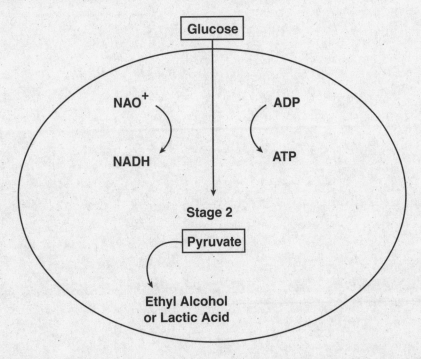

Until now, you have only read about the use of carbohydrates, namely glucose, as a source of fuel for cellular respiration. But it's important to remember that other macromolecules (lipids, proteins, and nucleic acids) can also be broken down to produce ATP.

VARIABLES AFFECTING THE RATE OF CELLULAR RESPIRATION

The rate of cellular respiration is regulated by the amount of ATP available in the cell through feedback inhibition. When there are high levels of ATP within the cell, ATP molecules bind to specific key enzymes that are directly involved in the production of ATP molecules. By binding to an enzyme, ATP shuts down the enzyme's ability to make additional ATP molecules. As ATP concentrations drop within the cell, the bond between ATP and the key enzyme is broken, thereby releasing the ATP molecule and allowing the enzyme to again engage in the production of ATP molecules.

REVIEW FOR LESSON 4

Take a few moments to practice test-taking strategies for questions about photosynthesis and cellular respiration. The answers and explanations are on page 42.

1 **What does the process of photosynthesis produce?**

   A Glycine, which is metabolized into less complex molecules by dehydration synthesis

   B Glycerol, which is metabolized into less complex molecules by dehydration synthesis

   C Glycogen, which is metabolized into more complex molecules by dehydration synthesis

   D Glucose, which is metabolized into more complex molecules by dehydration synthesis

2 **In most plants, the process of photosynthesis occurs most rapidly in plants that are exposed to equal intensities of—**

   F blue and yellow light

   G red and blue light

   H green and orange light

   J orange and yellow light

3 **The raw materials used by green plants for photosynthesis are—**

   A oxygen and carbon dioxide

   B glucose and water

   C sunlight and glucose

   D carbon dioxide and water

4 **Glucose is stored in plants in the form of—**

   F glycogen

   G starch

   H sucrose

   J glycerol

5 **Which organelle is the site of cellular respiration?**

   A Nucleus

   B Ribosomes

   C Mitochondrion

   D Endoplasmic reticulum

6 **The energy released from the anaerobic respiration of a glucose molecule is less than that released from the aerobic respiration of a glucose molecule because—**

   F yeast carry out anaerobic respiration and these organisms aren't as numerous as aerobic organisms

   G fewer bonds of the glucose molecule are broken during anaerobic respiration than during aerobic respiration

   H anaerobic respiration requires more enzymes than aerobic respiration

   J anaerobic respiration uses more oxygen than aerobic respiration

ANSWERS AND EXPLANATIONS

1 **D Glucose, which is metabolized into more complex molecules by dehydration synthesis.** Photosynthesis is the biochemical process that converts solar energy into chemical energy and produces glucose and oxygen. **A** and **B** are false because dehydration synthesis joins simple molecules together making more complex molecules. **C** is a storage form of converted glucose in animal tissue.

2 **G red and blue light.** Now, the question is really asking what the optimal wavelengths for photosynthesis to take place are. **F** is wrong because yellow light is not absorbed at the same rate as red. **H** is wrong because green light is reflected. **J** is wrong because orange and yellow light have lower rates of absorption than both blue and red light.

3 **D carbon dioxide and water.** In this case, you are looking for the reactants in photosynthesis. **A**, **B**, and **C** are all products formed as a result of photosynthesis.

4 **G starch.** Do you remember the potato test in lab class? In that experiment, you had to drop iodine on a sample of potato. A drop of iodine on a potato turns blueish black, indicating the presence of starch. **F** is wrong because glycogen is the storage form of converted glucose found in animal tissue, including the liver. **H** and **J** are not storage compounds.

5 **C Mitochondrion. A** is wrong because the nucleus houses chromosomes. Ribosomes, **B**, are the sites of protein synthesis. The endoplasmic reticulum, **D**, transports proteins and lipids.

6 **G fewer bonds of the glucose molecule are broken during anaerobic respiration than during aerobic respiration**. This question sounds a little intimidating, but all it is really asking is why anaerobic respiration produces less ATP (energy) than aerobic respiration. As you know, energy is released when chemical bonds are broken. The more bonds that are broken, the more energy that is released. **F** is not relevant. **H** and **J** are not true.

LESSON 5
THE CELL

BACK IN THE DAY

During the sixteenth and eighteenth centuries, scientists developed the **cell theory.** According to the theory, cells are the basic unit of structure and function in all living things. A cell is also the smallest unit of living material that can carry out all the activities necessary to sustain life. Of course, the development of cell theory had to wait until scientists could prove the existence of cells.

In 1665, Englishman **Robert Hooke,** using a primitive microscope, first observed a sample of cork and found small compartments that he called "cells." Hooke's work was followed by that of Dutch scientist **Anton van Leeuwenhoek.** In the late 1600s, van Leeuwenhoek reported the discovery of microscopic life based on his observation of samples from various sources, such as pond water and his own teeth.

As the resolving power of microscopes improved, so did scientific observations of microscopic and macroscopic organisms. In 1838, **Matthias Schleiden** concluded that embryonic plants were derived from a single cell and that all plant tissues were actually collections of cells. Similarly, in 1839, **Theodor Schwann** reported that animals were also collections of cells organized into tissues. Based on the available evidence, Schwann concluded that all organisms consisted of one or more cells.

Rudolf von Virchow rounded out the cell theory in 1858 when he observed that new cells were not the result of spontaneous generation, but rather they were the result of cell division. These observations led von Virchow to conclude that *all* cells were derived from preexisting ones.

With the groundbreaking discoveries of these researchers and the development of the electron microscope, biologists were finally able to figure out not only what type of cells exist, but also what happens *inside* them.

INTRODUCING THE PROKARYOTES

Prokaryotes are small, single-celled organisms that lack internal membrane-bound organelles. Simply stated, prokaryotes are molecules surrounded by a membrane and a cell wall.

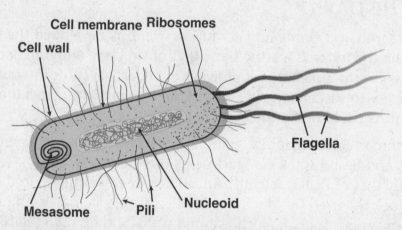

The cytoplasm contains the necessary proteins, fats, enzymes, and carbohydrates. In order to reproduce, these simple creatures undergo binary fission, where the cell divides in half, forming two cells that are smaller duplicates of each other. The most common examples of prokaryotes are bacteria and cyanobacteria (formerly known as blue-green algae).

Although prokaryotes are simple critters, their importance to the biological world should not be underestimated. They are among the oldest living organisms—going back nearly 3.5 billion years! These simple organisms have provided scientists with an invaluable tool for investigating and understanding the world around them. More on that later.

HERE'S SOMETHING FAMILIAR: THE EUKARYOTIC CELL

Eukaryotic organisms come in all shapes and sizes, ranging from the tiny *Paramecium* to the largest animal on Earth today, the blue whale. Regardless of the organism in which they reside, the cells of eukaryotic organisms all share the same general structural characteristics.

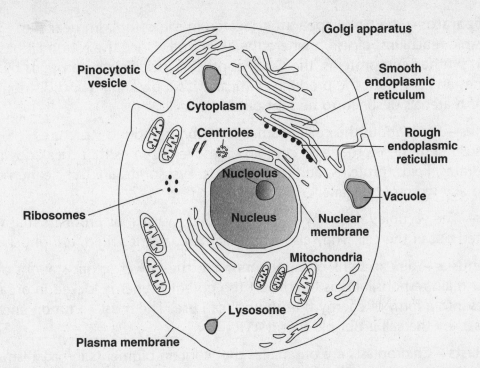

First and foremost, eukaryotic cells are characterized by the presence of membrane-bound organelles including a **nucleus,** a specialized compartment that houses the genetic information of the cell. The fact that eukaryotic cells contain special compartments for each of their organelles allows them to carry out a wider array of functions than their prokaryotic counterparts.

Here's a list of the organelles found in most eukaryotic cells.

Nucleus—The nucleus is the command center of the cell. It not only directs the inner workings of the cell, it also enables the cell to reproduce. It is here that the cell's DNA is located and where proteins are organized into **chromosomes,** which carry genes that direct cellular activities.

Nucleolus—A small organelle located inside the nucleus that aids in the synthesis of ribosomes.

Ribosomes—Small, membrane-bound organelles located in the cytoplasm. Their job is to help manufacture the proteins required by the cell. The ribosomes are round structures composed of RNA and proteins. They float freely throughout the cell or are associated with another structure called the endoplasmic reticulum.

Endoplasmic reticulum—The endoplasmic reticulum, or ER, is a network of membrane-bound canals that transports lipids and protein products to other locations within the cell. When the ER is bumpy or studded with ribosomes, it's called **rough ER.** Proteins manufactured on rough ER are marked to be transported out of the cell. When ER lacks ribosomes, it's called, you guessed it, **smooth ER.**

Golgi apparatus—The Golgi apparatus, located in the cytoplasm near the endoplasmic reticulum, picks up where the ER left off. Once the rough ER has done its part in synthesizing proteins, the Golgi apparatus modifies the proteins by the use of enzymes and sorts out the products. Basically, it's a packaging and distribution center for materials destined to be sent out of the cell.

Lysosomes—Throughout the cell are small, membrane-bound structures called lysosomes. These organelles contain digestive enzymes that break down carbohydrates, lipids, proteins, and nucleic acids. Lysosomes are the cleanup crew, removing any worn-out organelles or debris.

Vacuoles—The vacuoles store any macromolecules, wastes, or products that will be transported out of the cell. They also help maintain a plant's rigid, upright shape.

Mitochondria—You can think of mitochondria as the power or gas stations of the cell. Their main responsibility is to convert the potential energy locked in organic molecules into a form of energy that the cell can use. The most common energy source used by the cell is our old friend **ATP**.

Chloroplasts—Chloroplasts are organelles that contain pigments in organisms such as green plants and algae. The chloroplasts play a key role in both photosynthesis and carbohydrate production, and they contain unique genetic material.

Centrioles—The centrioles are cylinder-shaped organelles that are found near the nucleus. Their role is to assist in cellular division. When the cell is ready to divide, the centrioles produce special fibers called **spindle fibers,** which help in separating chromosomes and moving them to opposite ends of the cell. Keep in mind that *only* animal cells have centrioles.

Cytoplasm—The cytoplasm is the medium inside the cell in which organelles are suspended; kind of like the glue that holds everything together. It also contains protein fibers that assist in cell division and help maintain the cell's shape.

Plasma membrane—The plasma membrane is a phospholipid bilayer that surrounds a cell to separate its contents from the surrounding environment.

Cell wall—The cell wall is a rigid structure found in some eukaryotic organisms, such as plants, fungi, and algae. Its job is to surround the cell membrane and protect its contents. The cell wall is composed mostly of cellulose in plants and algae and chitin in fungi.

PLANT CELLS VS. ANIMAL CELLS

Plants and animals are both part of the eukaryotic family. Each is a multicellular organism and shares most of the organelles described previously. However, plant cells contain a tough cell wall and chloroplasts. Each chloroplast contains chlorophyll, the light capturing pigment that gives plants their green color. Another difference between plant and animal cells is that most of the space within a plant cell is taken up by a huge vacuole.

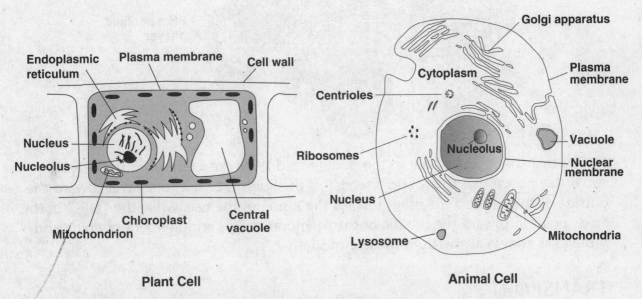

Plant Cell   Animal Cell

Here's what is known about prokaryotes and eukaryotes:

Structure	Prokaryotes	Plant Cells	Animal Cells
Cell wall	Yes	Yes	No
Plasma membrane	Yes	Yes	Yes
Organelles	No	Yes	Yes
Nucleus	No	Yes	Yes
Centrioles	No	No	Yes
Example	**Bacteria**	**Cactus**	**Human**

Modelling the Cell Membrane

Although the plasma membrane appears to be a simple, thin layer that surrounds the cell, it's actually a complex structure made up of proteins and two layers of **phospholipids.**

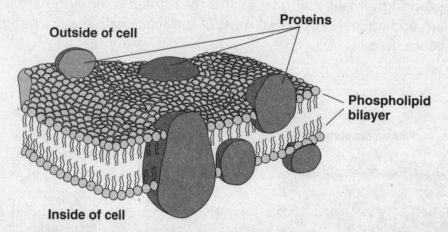

Notice that the proteins float in the double-lipid layer like icebergs in the ocean. You'll also notice that the round "heads" of the lipids face out; one layer toward the outside of the cell and the other toward the inside of the cell, while the "tails" of the lipids point in toward the middle of the membrane. This arrangement of lipids and proteins is known as the **fluid-mosaic model.**

TRANSPORT

Okay, now that you know what the cell membrane is made of, how do substances move into and out of the membrane?

Diffusion

Some substances move across the membrane by **simple diffusion**. If there's a high concentration of a substance outside the cell and a low concentration inside the cell, then the substance moves into the cell. Simple diffusion is also known as **passive transport,** because this type of movement requires no energy to be used.

Remember: The cell membrane is made partly of lipids. Simple diffusion or passive transport only works if the material that "wants" to get into the cell is soluble in lipids (a condition called lipid soluble).

Facilitated Diffusion

One important type of passive transport is called **facilitated diffusion.** In this case, various molecules can get past the cell membrane even if they are *not* lipid soluble. How? Well, remember our discussion of the proteins in the fluid-mosaic model? Special proteins called **carrier proteins** can help lipid-insoluble substances get across the cell membrane. These carrier proteins shuttle certain molecules and ions across the membrane and against the concentration gradient.

Facilitated diffusion and simple diffusion have two important similarities: Both allow a molecule to get into the cell if its concentration outside is higher than its concentration inside. The opposite is also true: Whenever there is a higher concentration of a substance inside a cell than outside, the substance moves out of the cell. The key point to remember is that no matter what the position (inside or outside the cell), the *direction of movement always has to go from higher to lower,* or *down* a concentration gradient. Therefore, both simple and facilitated diffusion do not require energy.

So, what is known about passive transport?

> **TIP: Osmosis** is the special term applied to the movement of **water** molecules across the cell membrane (as a result of diffusion).

It is also known as **diffusion.**

Substances move from a region of higher concentration to one of lower concentration along a concentration gradient.

Facilitated diffusion is a unique type of passive transport in which a membrane (carrier) protein is used to shuttle ions and molecules across the membrane.

Both facilitated diffusion and simple diffusion do *not* require energy.

ACTIVE TRANSPORT

Suppose a substance wants to move in the opposite direction—from an area of *lower* concentration to an area of *higher* concentration. Then what? Well, first and foremost, this type of transport requires energy. **Active transport,** as the phrase implies, is any process that requires the use of energy in order to move substances across the cell membrane against the concentration gradient. Basically, molecules are moved from an area of lower concentration of molecules or ions to an area of higher concentration of molecules. But where does the cell get this energy? From proteins in the cell membrane powered by ATP. A special protein called the sodium-potassium pump or ion pump starts the chain of events. The pump moves sodium ions out of the cell and potassium ions into the cell. The pump depends on ATP to get the ions across the membrane.

More on active transport

Cells, particularly unicellular organisms, have several other tricks up their proverbial sleeves that help them move particles too large to cross the membrane. The following forms of transport are energy-requiring processes and, therefore, are forms of active transport:

- **Pinocytosis ("Cell-drinking")**—In this process, vacuoles form at the surface of the cell membrane. They then suck in substances on the cell surface and transport them into the cell to be digested.
- **Phagocytosis ("Cell-Eating")**—A process in which large food particles are engulfed by the cell and brought into the cell for intracellular digestion.

KEEPING UP THE DIALOGUE: CELL COMMUNICATION

Cell communication is important to the function of the whole organism. The nervous and endocrine systems are responsible for moving messages from cell to cell. Nerve cells accomplish this task through the actions of special molecules called **neurotransmitters.** Neurotransmitters bind to specific receptor proteins on a cell's surface, causing physical, chemical, or electrical changes in the cell membrane and cytoplasm. The resulting chemical change in the cytoplasm allows for a momentary opening of channels through the cell membrane or the production of secondary cytoplasmic messenger molecules.

Endocrine cells also secrete a special type of chemical messenger molecule called a **hormone.** Hormones are stable molecules with specific shapes. This means that specific hormones only bind to specific receptor proteins. Some hormones, such as peptide hormones, join with a receptor protein that initiates a change in cytoplasmic components and the production of secondary cytoplasmic messenger molecules. Other hormones, such as steroid hormones, pass through the cell membrane and stick to cytoplasmic protein receptors, which then transport the hormones into the nucleus, where the hormones affect the cell's activity.

A quick word on viruses

It's important to point out that viruses manage to exist without the full array of cellular components that make up even the simplest life-forms. Viruses are composites of organic compounds consisting of a short segment of nucleic acids, most often DNA, surrounded by a protein coat called a **capsid.** Once they infect a cell, viruses harness and utilize the DNA-replication machinery of the infected cell to reproduce their own nucleic acid strand. Unlike prokaryotic and eukaryotic cells, viruses are unable to replicate on their own. Because of their lack of cellular components and their inability to reproduce with other viruses, the scientific community does not view viruses as living organisms.

REVIEW FOR LESSON 5

Take a few moments to practice test-taking strategies for questions about cell theory. The answers and explanations are on page 52.

1 In an amoeba, the structures formed as a result of the ingestion of yeast cells are known as—

    A cytoplasm

    B food vacuoles

    C golgi apparatus

    D endoplasmic reticulum

2 A major difference between plant cells and animals cells is that plant cells have—

    F cell membranes

    G mitochondria

    H cell walls

    J vacuoles

3 Some scientists disagree on whether viruses are alive. Which of the following supports the position that viruses are not alive?

    A Viruses cannot manufacture their own food.

    B Viruses are not composed of cells.

    C Viruses do not contain nucleic acids.

    D Viruses do not contain the element carbon.

4 A student observed a green plant cell under the low-power objective of her microscope and noted the movement of organelles as shown in diagram A. She then added three drops of 10 percent saline solution to the slide and observed the cell as shown in diagram B.

    A   *B*

What process is illustrated in the diagrams?

    F Osmosis

    G Cyclosis

    H Pinocytosis

    J Phagocytosis

5 Which of the following is *not* a method of moving materials across cell membranes without using energy?

    A Passive transport

    B Facilitated diffusion

    C Osmosis

    D Active transport

ANSWERS AND EXPLANATIONS

1 **B   food vacuoles. A, C,** and **D** are not transient cellular components formed when the need arises.

2 **H   cell walls.** Plant cells, unlike animal cells, contain cell walls. Plant cells and animal cells are both eukaryotic. **F, G,** and **J** are all membrane-bound organelles found in both plant cells and animal cells.

3 **B   Viruses are not composed of cells. A** is true, but heterotrophs can't manufacture their own food either. Viruses contain nucleic acids and little else, so **C** is false. Viruses contain both proteins and nucleic acids. These compounds both contain carbon, so **D** is false.

4 **F   Osmosis.** The cell in diagram *A* looks like a normal plant cell that has chloroplasts located near the cell membrane, which is next to the cell wall. In diagram *B*, the membrane and chloroplasts are in the middle of the cell. In order for the cell membrane to pull away, the liquid in the cell must have left the cell. Water enters and leaves the cell through osmosis. **CYC**losis, **G,** is the **CYC**ling of material around the inside of the cell. **PIN**ocytosis, **H,** is the movement of larger particles into the cell by vesicles **PIN**ched off at the surface. Pha**G**ocytosis, **J,** moves large molecules into the cell by en**G**ulfing them.

5 **D   Active transport.** Active transport requires ATP because it involves movement of materials against a concentration gradient (from higher to lower concentration). Materials can be transported across a plasma membrane in a variety of ways. Passive transport (diffusion), osmosis, and facilitated transport do not require energy because the materials move down a concentration gradient.

LESSON 6
LIFE AT THE SYSTEMS AND ORGANISMS LEVEL

HOW'D THEY DO THAT?

The fact that organisms have changed through time is nothing new. Even in the nineteenth century, scientists were pretty confident that organisms went through a series of changes to arrive at their present form. What they didn't know is *how* they performed those changes.

> **Taxonomy**—the study of the general principles of scientific classification. A taxonomist is a scientist who deals with the description, identification, naming and classification of organisms.

In 1809, **Jean Baptiste de Lamarck** published *Philosophie Zoologique* (Zoological Philosophy), in which he proposed that rather than changing by unseen forces, organisms change in response to their needs in a given environment. Basically, organisms would adapt to their environment, and then pass these acquired characteristics to their offspring. For example, Lamarck said that giraffes had long necks because they were constantly reaching for higher leaves while feeding and that future giraffes would have longer necks as a result.

By the mid-1830s, the scientific community was divided on the issue of the Lamarckian theory of use and disuse or, as one might say now, "use it or lose it." **Charles Darwin** dismissed the popular theory and continued to search for other explanations. Darwin read **Thomas Robert Malthus's** *Essay on the Principles of Populations*. Malthus's theory was that populations increase faster than the environment's ability to support them, creating a struggle for existence. Darwin adapted Malthus's struggle for existence principle and applied it to plant and animal species, arriving at the theory of **natural selection.** Interestingly, another English naturalist, **Alfred Russel Wallace,** who had also read Malthus's essay, independently arrived at the same conclusion. In 1859, Darwin published his theory of natural selection in *On the Origin of Species by Means of Natural Selection*. This work revolutionized the fields of evolution and taxonomy.

THE TIE THAT BINDS

To find structural similarities between all living organisms, you'd have to look very closely at the contents of their cells. Prokaryotic (monerans) and eukaryotic (protists, fungi, plants, and animals) find common ground in a few of their cellular structures. **All** cells have some sort of genetic material responsible for passing hereditary information from one generation to the next. **All** cells have a cell membrane that surrounds the contents of the cell, ribosomes that facilitate protein production, and cytoplasm. Beyond these similarities, each of the major classifications of organisms hopscotches around sharing similarities with some groups, while developing other characteristics that are uniquely their own.

MONERANS

Monerans are divided into two kingdoms: **archaebacteria** and **eubacteria.** Even though monerans share a few structural characteristics with plants and fungi, such as cell walls, monerans clearly do not belong to either group. Without a nuclear membrane, the genetic material in these single-celled organisms floats freely in the cytoplasm. Additionally, the molecular structure of the cell walls in monerans is unlike the cell walls of either plants or fungi. The cell walls of eubacteria contain a starchlike composition. The cell walls of archaebacteria are made of lipids not found in any other organism. That pretty much sums up the structural uniqueness of monerans.

PROTISTS

Unlike monerans, which are always unicellular, protists come in *both* unicellular and multicellular varieties. Protists appear to be the first group of organisms in which **motile** (able to move) species are characterized by flagella and cilia, with the 9 + 2 structure of microtubules, that are extensions of cytoplasm and its structural components.

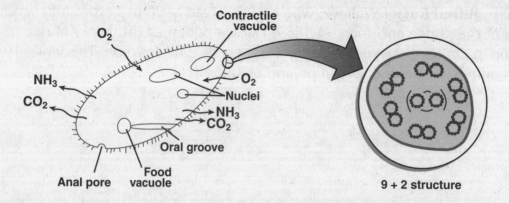

9 + 2 structure

The 9 + 2 structure is found in all eukaryotic cells that have these organelles. This group is a kind of hodgepodge because some protists have chloroplasts and are autotrophic, i.e., green algae. Others, such as amoebas, are predators that hunt down prey. Still, other protists ingest their food as fungi do. Therefore, taxonomists designated the term protists for all eukaryotic organisms that cannot be classified based on physical structures, cellular structures, or metabolic processes as those in plants, animals, or fungi.

FUN-GUY

Fungi represent the first group of organisms to display multicellularity *and* cell specialization, an innovation over multicellular protists. Once lumped in with the plants, taxonomists split fungi from plants when it became apparent the fungi had much less in common with plants than was previously thought. The cell walls of fungi contain **chitin,** a compound that serves to distinguish fungi from species of any other kingdom.

Fungi are also characterized by structures called **hyphae,** long slender filaments made of strings of cells. Hyphae are structurally unique among eukaryotes. The cells of hyphae are not completely separated from one another, so this leads to the formation of incomplete **septa** between the cells that permit the flow of cytoplasm and cellular organelles from one cell to the next. This open-door policy also allows nutrients to move rapidly throughout the organism, particularly to the rapidly growing tips. A collection of hyphae is called **mycelium,** and it provides fungi with a large absorptive surface through which to obtain nutrients.

PLANTS

Plants are multicellular organisms that share some structural characteristics with other kingdoms, such as membrane-bound organelles (eukaryotes), cell walls (bacteria, fungi), and photosynthetic pigments (bacteria, protists), but they also have many specialized structures and tissues of their own. Some unique plant structures include cells and tissues that function in the transport of water and nutrients, specialized photosynthetic structures, structures used in the uptake of water and nutrients, and the production of flowers, fruits, and seeds. Many **terrestrial** plants also produce structures and compounds used in defense.

ANIMALS

By now you've probably noticed that animals and other organisms have a lot of common structures. But keep in mind that even though they share similar structures, animals are clearly distinguishable from other kingdoms. What makes them different?

- The absence of cell walls makes animal cells different from cells of other kingdoms.
- Specialized cells organized into tissues and organ systems for the purpose of carrying out specialized functions is limited to animals and plants as is the production of specialized chemical messenger molecules called **hormones.**
- Animals are uniquely characterized by a body cavity (**coelom**), **segmentation,** and **appendages.** Many animals have also developed specialized structures and pigmentation that allow them to be successful in the **niches** that they occupy.

METABOLISM

Metabolism is the sum of all chemical reactions that are carried out in an organism. Just about anything an organism does—grow, develop, eat, and breathe—results in chemical reactions that require energy. Here's a closer look at how different organisms carry out their daily life functions.

FOOD FOR THOUGHT

MONERANS

Bacteria can actually be divided into three groups depending on how they obtain their energy.

- **Autotrophic** bacteria are photosynthetic bacteria that obtain energy from sunlight. However, because they are prokaryotic, they do not have membrane-bound organelles, including chloroplasts. Instead, photosynthetic pigments are located within their cell membranes. These little organisms made all the original oxygen on Earth. Without them, animals would not exist.
- **Chemotrophic** bacteria obtain energy by removing electrons from inorganic compounds, such as ammonia, NH_3, and methane, CH_4. Many of these form the basis of food chains in the deep sea and underground. Nitrogen fixing bacteria, which live in the roots of special plants called **legumes**, convert atmospheric nitrogen into a form easily utilized by plants. Soybean, pea, and clover plants are all examples of legumes.
- **Heterotrophic** bacteria absorb organic material produced by other organisms and feed on other microorganisms. Together with fungi, bacteria are important **decomposers** that unlock nutrients found in dead organisms and organic matter. To sum up, decomposers recycle nutrient molecules making them available to other organisms.

PROTISTS

Protists have come up with a number of ways to get their energy. Autotrophic protists, such as unicellular green algae, use chloroplasts and photosynthetic pigments to harness the energy from sunlight, making organic compounds and ATP.

Heterotrophic protists such as *Amoeba* and *Paramecium* are active hunters. *Paramecium*, for example, uses its cilia to move food into an opening called an **oral groove.** Once the food has been digested, wastes are excreted through an **anal pore.** *Amoeba,* on the other hand, surrounds its food with flexible extensions of its body know as pseudopodia. These tiny armlike structures reach out, close around a chunk of food, and gather it into a forming **food vacuole.** This food vacuole acts like a tiny stomach; it contains digestive enzymes that break down the food particles. The vacuole then recombines with the cell membrane, squirting the waste products out into the environment through phagocytosis.

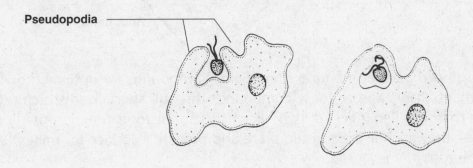

Pseudopodia

FUNGI

As you learned earlier, fungi are also important decomposers and nutrient recyclers. All fungi are heterotrophic. They secrete enzymes that break down decaying or dead organic matter, which they then absorb.

PLANTS

Plants are autotrophic organisms that use sunlight and carbon dioxide in the process of photosynthesis. The leaves of plants house the chloroplasts and photosynthetic pigments, which are crucial to photosynthesis. Leaf structure must accomplish several tasks at once. Not only does it need to provide an adequate surface area for photosynthesis to take place, a leaf must also regulate or limit the amount of water loss without limiting gas exchange.

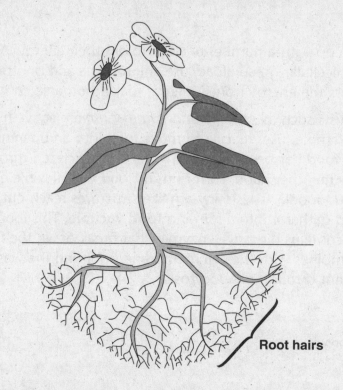

Root hairs

Plants also need trace elements and inorganic compounds for optimal growth and development. Plants absorb these compounds through specialized structures called roots, or **rhizoids**. Regardless of their exact structures, roots function pretty much the same—they anchor the plant in place and provide a surface for mineral and water absorption.

ANIMALS

More complex organisms don't have it as easy as unicellular organisms. Because multicellular organisms, such as animals, cannot absorb food across their cell membrane, they have evolved a variety of ways to obtain their nutrients. Animals possess what is thought of as a proper digestive tract, in which food is digested through extracellular digestion. That is, food is digested in specialized cavities, then transported to the cells.

More Complex Life-Forms

In an earthworm, the food passes through several specialized regions of the gut: **mouth, esophagus, crop** (a storage organ), **gizzard** (a grinding organ), **intestine,** and **anus.**

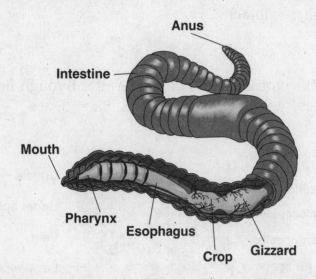

By the time food has passed through all the different parts of the earthworm's gut, it has been thoroughly digested. Grasshoppers, which are arthropods, have a similar digestive system.

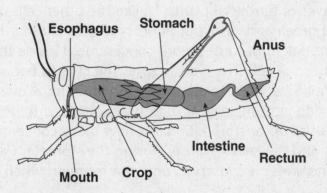

In addition to the organs pictured above, grasshoppers also have **salivary glands** (which secrete saliva) and **gastric caeca** (which contain digestive enzymes). These specialized organs enable the grasshopper to digest its food more effectively.

Different organisms have diverse digestive systems. Cows, for example, have four stomachs! However, few digestive systems are understood as well as the human digestive system. You will learn more about the human digestive system in Lesson 7.

GAS EXCHANGE

MONERANS

Without specialized cells and structures, monerans are limited to gas exchange directly through cell membranes.

PROTISTS

Simple organisms like protists get rid of toxic wastes through simple diffusion, which releases these wastes into the environment.

PLANTS

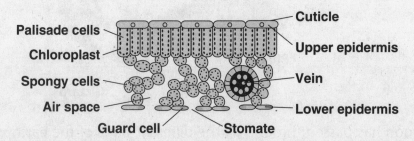

Palisade cells — Chloroplast — Spongy cells — Air space — Guard cell — Stomate — Cuticle — Upper epidermis — Vein — Lower epidermis

Stomata are structures charged with regulating the amount of oxygen, carbon dioxide, and water that enter and leave a leaf. Stomata are usually found on the underside of the leaves of terrestrial plants. Unlike the other cells on the bottom of a leaf, **guard cells** are green and carry out photosynthesis. During the daytime, this is exactly what they do. Sugar becomes more concentrated inside the cell than outside causing water to enter the cell. The water causes the cells to become shorter and fatter opening the holes between them called stomata. This allows water and oxygen out and carbon dioxide into the leaf. At nighttime, photosynthesis stops and the sugar in the cells is used up or stored. Sugar is now more concentrated outside the cell, so water leaves and the cells collapse, closing the stomata. Carbon dioxide isn't needed anymore, and water is conserved until the morning when the process starts all over again.

ANIMALS

With few exceptions, animals are characterized by the organization of cells into tissues that carry out gas exchange functions. The types of tissues and organs used for this purpose is determined by the nature of the environment in which the organism lives. While simple **invertebrates,** such as earthworms, diffuse oxygen and carbon dioxide directly across their outer coverings, larger organisms like fish, reptiles, birds, and mammals have evolved gills or lungs to deal with gas exchange in their specific environments.

GETTING THINGS WHERE THEY NEED TO GO: TRANSPORT

MONERANS

Transport in bacteria isn't any more complicated than transport in any single cell. The cell membrane acts as a barrier, using active and passive transport to get things into the cell.

PROTISTS

In the single-celled protists, transport happens just like in monerans. Active and passive transport through the cell membrane is enough to do the job. However, there is a limit to how big a cell can get before this no longer works. The amount of gas, food, and water that can diffuse into or out of a cell depends on its surface area. Unfortunately, as a cell grows its surface area never grows as quickly as its volume. Pretty soon the cell gets too big in volume to get enough material through the cell membrane fast enough. That is why you never see cells the size of chickens.

FUNGI

You learned that most fungi have cells that are interconnected. They use this structural feature to increase their ability to transport gases and nutrients into and out of the organism. They still rely on active and passive transport to accomplish their goals.

PLANTS

Simple plants, such as mosses and lichens, do not have any specialized tissues for transport. They remain small and live in moist environments like marshes or swamps, where they can rely on active and passive transport to get the water and nutrients to all the cells.

But that is just not good enough if you want to be a tree. Ferns, gymnosperms (flowerless, seed-bearing land plants, i.e., pine trees), and angiosperms (flowering plants) all have specialized tissues that carry materials upward toward the leaves and down toward the roots. In general, these are called **vascular tissues.**

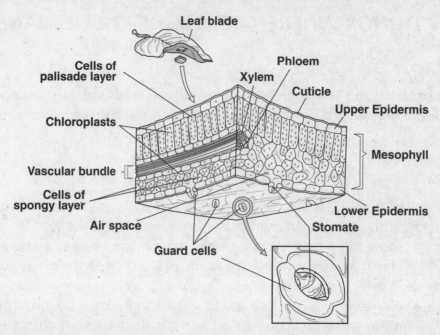

One material that the plant has to move is water. It takes in water and inorganic compounds through single-celled root hairs, and then allows it to diffuse into specialized cells called **xylem.** You can think about xylem as the plant's internal elevator, bringing water up in a continuous column to each leaf. As it is used up in photosynthesis or when it evaporates from the leaves, it exerts a constant pull on the xylem cells that keep the water flowing.

The sugars and starches made in the leaves also have to move around to the rest of the plant. How do they do that? Well, plants utilize special cells called **phloem,** which help transport these compounds. They move the sugar and starches downward and into the rest of the plant. The fluid that flows through the phloem cells is often called **sap.** An easy way to remember the difference between xylem and phloem is the saying: **Xylem up, Phloem down.**

The third specialized cell is called **vascular cambium,** and it is responsible for making new xylem and phloem cells. It is usually located in the ring right under the bark of a tree. Xylem cells are made on the inside of this tissue and make up most of the wood of the tree. Phloem cells are made just on the outside of this layer. This is why carving your initials into a tree trunk is not a good idea. If you cut through the bark, you will probable cut some of the phloem and cambium. If it is cut too deep or too often, the tree will die.

ANIMALS

Simple animals don't have too much trouble with transport. They just slosh in and out of water and let active and passive transport do the rest. But what if you live on land or get too large? Your only choice would be to develop some special structures for carrying material. In animals, this is called a circulatory system.

Circulatory systems consist of vessels that carry fluid and sometimes a pump to help keep that fluid moving. Some systems are called **open circulatory systems.** This means that the fluid collected in a vessel is pumped into the body cavity and distributed all over, keeping the other body cells well supplied. The fluid then flows back down to the bottom of the animal and is repumped around. In grasshoppers, for example, blood is pumped by the heart through vessels that open into large spaces know as sinuses.

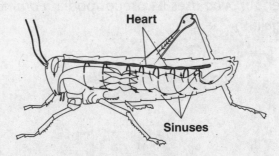

Open circulatory system of a grasshopper

Other animals, humans included, have **closed circulatory systems.** In this type of system, all the fluid is contained *inside* the vessels. A pump keeps the fluid moving throughout the vessels and around the body where active and passive transport are used. The earthworm is an example of an organism that has a closed circulatory system.

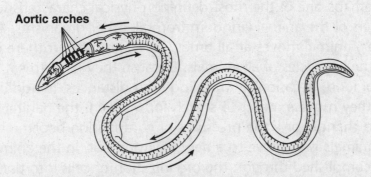

Closed circulatory system of an earthworm

As you can see from the diagram above, earthworms have five **aortic arches** that pump blood through the body.

ON THE MOVE: LOCOMOTION

MONERANS

Some monerans, such as bacteria, employ flagella and cilia to assist their movements from place to place. It is important to remember that these structures are unlike similar structures found in eukaryotes. In monerans, flagella and cilia are *not* extensions of cytoplasm with the associated microtubules and microfilaments. Instead, they are projections of the cell membrane and are composed of proteins and lipids.

PROTISTS

Flagella and cilia appear in this group as a way of helping them move from place to place. As you read earlier, *Amoeba* uses its pseudopodia; *Paramecium*, its cilia; and *Euglena*, its whiplike flagellum.

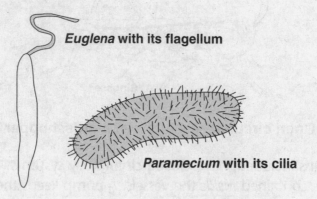

Euglena with its flagellum

Paramecium with its cilia

ANIMALS

Locomotion is perhaps one of the most defining physical characteristics that separates members of the animal kingdom from all other organisms. Although it's true that not every animal moves at all times, for the most part there is at least one mobile stage in the life cycles of all animals. Because they have to eat, animals often move in search of food, occasionally traveling long distances. In addition to their search for food, they move in order to search for mates. If the habitat becomes unsuitable due to change, or if the pressures of competition become too great, one option open to animals is to move to a new environment. In the animal kingdom, locomotion is accomplished through the organization of cells into tissues and structures that propel organisms in a desired direction.

REPRODUCTION

Yes, reproduction is considered a crucial life function for the organism as well as for the good of the species. In the following section, terms like meiosis and mitosis will appear. For the moment, just remember that each is a method of reproduction. You will learn more about the specifics of meiosis and mitosis in Lesson 8.

MONERANS

You know that as a rule it's good to avoid sweeping generalities such as *all*, *always*, and *never*. However, when discussing prokaryotic reproductive strategies, it's fairly safe to say that this group of organisms is about as energetically conservative as they get. Remember, monerans reproduce asexually by binary fission. Each new cell produced is genetically identical to the parent cell.

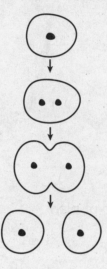

PROTISTS

Whereas monerans reproduce asexually through binary fission, some flexibility and the emergence of sexual reproduction begin to occur in this first kingdom of eukaryotes. The number of cells a protist has does not necessarily indicate the reproductive strategy that it uses. Many unicellular protists such as *Amoeba* reproduce asexually through mitosis. However, under certain environmental conditions, some unicellular protists may switch between asexual and sexual modes of reproduction.

FUNGI

Fungi are host to several unique processes, including nuclear mitosis and shared nuclei, during sexual reproduction. In fungi, mitosis occurs almost exclusively by dividing the nucleus. During asexual reproduction, mitosis leads to the production of **haploid** (*n*) spores formed in the reproductive structures at the tips of **hyphae.** Wind may carry spores ejected from these structures great distances before the spores land and germinate, forming new fungal hypha.

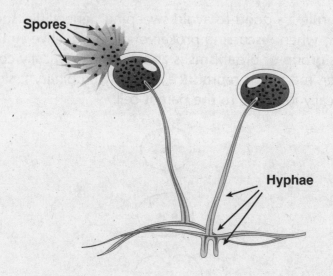

PLANTS

Here's a look at your everyday type of plant.

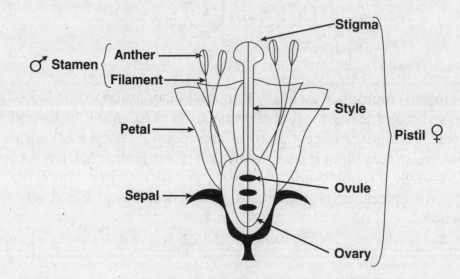

The male parts of the flower are collectively called the **stamen,** while the female parts are collectively called the **pistil.** The **sepals** are the green, leaflike structures that cover and protect the flower (primarily before it has blossomed, when it covers the entire bud). The petals are usually brightly colored in order to attract potential pollinators.

The Stamen

The stamen consists of the anther and the filament. The **anther** is the structure that produces pollen grains. Pollen grains are the plant's male gametophytes, or sperm cells. Pollen grains are produced by the millions and lifted by the wind into the air; they are also picked up by bees. The **filament** is just the thin stalk that holds up the anther.

The Pistil

The **pistil** is made up of three structures: the stigma, the style, and the ovary. The **stigma** is the sticky portion of the pistil that captures the pollen grains as they fly through the air or as they are transported to the pistil by an insect. The **style** is the tubelike structure that connects the stigma with the ovary, and the **ovary** is the site of fertilization. Inside the ovaries are ovules, which contain the plant's equivalent of female gametophytes. Apples, pears, and oranges are all fertilized ovaries of flowering plants—no joke!

Flowering plants carry out a process called double fertilization. When a pollen grain lands on the stigma, it germinates and grows a thin pollen tube down through the style. The pollen grain divides into two sperm nuclei that descend through the pollen tube and into the ovary. One sperm nucleus ($1n$) fuses with an egg nucleus ($1n$) to form a zygote ($2n$). This zygote will eventually form a plant. The other sperm nucleus ($1n$) fuses with two polar nuclei ($2n$) in the ovary to form the endosperm, which ends up as food for the plant embryo. Double fertilization produces two things: a new plant and food for the plant embryo.

ANIMALS

Most animals carry out sexual reproduction in which males produce haploid gametes called sperm and females produce haploid gametes called eggs. Fertilization occurs when an egg and sperm cell fuse, producing a diploid zygote. There are two types of fertilization: internal and external. In some animals, the eggs and sperms are both forced out of the body and into the environment where they come together—usually by chance. This is called **external fertilization.** Only aquatic animals carry out external fertilization.

Other animals retain the eggs inside the female and the male deposits the sperm. This is called **internal fertilization**. She may then go on and lay her eggs outside her body, like reptiles and birds. If you are wondering about humans, you will read about human reproduction in Lesson 8. For now, just keep in mind that humans carry out internal fertilization.

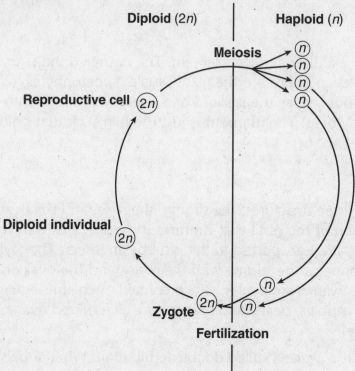

ORGANISMS AND THEIR ENVIRONMENT

MONERANS

Extreme environmental conditions, such as drought or high temperatures, causes some bacteria to form a thick-walled structure called an **endospore** around their DNA. Endospores are capable of producing new bacteria when the environment returns to a more favorable condition.

PROTISTS

Some protists, like the normally photosynthetic *Euglena*, can switch from autotrophic to heterotrophic modes of nutrition in response to an environmental change. Similarly, environmental stress may induce normally asexually reproducing organisms to switch to a sexual mode of reproduction.

FUNGI

Haploid spores produced by fungi will not grow in unsuitable environments. Instead, spores remain dormant until environmental conditions are favorable once again.

PLANTS

When the environment takes a turn for the worse, plants are usually the first indicators. Whether it's high or low temperatures, floods or drought, plants can't pack their bags and move on to friendlier climates. Instead, they have to cope. Therefore, many plants have strategies in place directed by hormones that allow them to accommodate environmental change.

What's a hormone again?

Earlier on, you read that a hormone was a chemical messenger molecule that sends specific signals to specific organs. Plants produce the following four major types of hormones in response to environmental cues:

1. **Auxins** are hormones produced in the tips and stems of plants that cause cells to elongate and grow fruit, delay fruit-and-leaf drop, and inhibit side buds from growing (apical dominance).
2. **Cytokinins** are hormones produced in the tips of roots that promote cell division and side-bud growth and inhibit leaf drop.
3. **Ethylene** is a gaseous growth factor that promotes fruit ripening, fruit flower, and leaf drop. It also fosters lateral bud growth.
4. **Gibberellins** are hormones that promote stem elongation and seed germination.

Plant responses to environmental change

Tropism is a plant growth response either toward or away from an external stimulus.
- **Phototropism:** Auxins cause the side of a plant facing away from the light to grow faster and longer. This makes the plant bend toward the light.
- **Gravitotropism:** Auxins cause the roots to grow faster toward gravity and the shoots to grow faster away from it.
- **Thigmotropism:** Touch can cause plant cells to grow at different rates.

Photoperiodism is the way plants respond to changing ratios between light and dark periods; the duration of darkness stimulates the production of hormones that control flowering in plants.
- **Short-day plants:** plants (tulips, daffodils, strawberries) that flower in spring and fall when length of daylight is short relative to hours of darkness
- **Long-day plants:** plants (irises, clover, corn) that flower in summer when length of daylight is more than a critical period of light
- **Day-neutral plants:** plants that flower regardless of the relative periods of daylight and darkness

Dormancy is a plant response to changes in temperature and the availability of moisture. Woody perennial plants, such as lilacs, become inactive, stop growing, and form protective scales around buds when environmental conditions become unfavorable for growth. Herbaceous perennials store carbohydrates in underground stems and roots, allowing the shoot to die off. The production of seeds that remain dormant until favorable environmental conditions are present is yet another strategy for plant species to survive unfavorable environmental conditions.

ANIMALS

When faced with environment change, animals, perhaps more than any other group, move on to new pastures in order to secure necessary resources. Similar to perennial plants faced with cold periods, animals that are adapted to seasonal environmental change in terrestrial environments may weather the unfavorable conditions in a state of dormancy or hibernation. Hibernation is a typical survival strategy used by invertebrates, amphibians, reptiles, and a few mammals. The bodies of many mammals respond to impending seasonal cold periods as signaled by shorter-day lengths by storing extra fat and thickening hair.

EXCRETION

As you already know, all organisms must get rid of wastes, or metabolic by-products.

In simple organisms, such as prokaryotes and monerans, waste products diffuse out of these organisms at any point along the cell surface. Similarly, protists also lack specialized excretory structures, so they are reduced to using simple diffusion to remove any leftover water, salts, ammonia, and carbon dioxide. Metabolic wastes that are too large to diffuse out of protists are either stored in specialized vacuoles or removed through active transport.

Photosynthetic protists, such as algae and plants, recycle certain wastes generated from photosynthesis and cellular respiration. During the day, plants produce more oxygen than can be recycled, so excess oxygen and water vapor is released into the atmosphere through specialized structures called stomata. Refer to the section on gas exchange in this lesson to learn more about stomata.

ANIMALS

Animals have developed a number of ways to remove metabolic wastes. Hydras are small, multicellular animals that excrete wastes by simple diffusion. However, as the size, complexity, and environment of organisms change, so does their mechanisms for excretion.

Earthworms

The complex structure of an earthworm requires specialized excretory structures. Without a specialized organ system for gas exchange, carbon dioxide is released from blood vessels located just below the moist skin of earthworms.

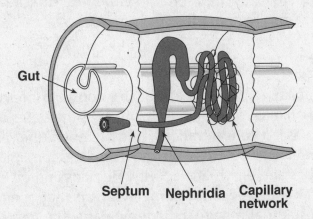

Carbon dioxide is released from earthworms as it diffuses out of blood, across moist skin, and into the surrounding environment. Nitrogenous wastes, salts, and water are collected in specialized structures called **nephridia,** which then exit through the pores of the skin.

Grasshoppers

The excretory systems of terrestrial invertebrates, such as grasshoppers, perform functions similar to those of earthworms, but with an added twist. Not only must their excretory systems eliminate wastes, but their systems must accomplish these tasks without losing too much water.

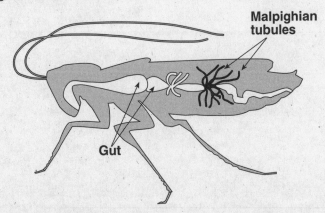

Malpighian tubules are specialized structures that concentrate nitrogenous wastes in the form of uric acid, salts, and small amounts of water. As these wastes are eliminated through the digestive tract, they are mixed with undigested food in the intestine. Any remaining water is reabsorbed and the semisolid waste exits the body through the anus.

The excretory systems of amphibians, reptiles, birds, and mammals must all perform excretory functions similar to those of insects: the elimination of metabolic wastes with minimal water loss. Each group of organisms has specialized organs that concentrate nitrogenous wastes and solid waste produced as a result of the digestive process. These wastes are eliminated through either the **cloaca** (amphibians, reptiles, birds) or through the **urethra** and **anus** (mammals).

HOMEOSTASIS

Homeostasis is the ability to maintain a relatively constant internal environment. For many plants and animals, including humans, that translates to making sure that conditions, such as ion concentrations, body temperature, pH of cell and body fluids, and rates of metabolic activities like growth, digestion, and excretion, are regulated by hormones and enzymatic activity. Humans and other animals maintain homeostasis through **negative-feedback mechanisms** that operate in a manner similar to the thermostat that monitors the temperature in your house during the winter. When the thermostat in your room falls below the temperature set, your heater kicks on. When the room reaches the set thermostatic temperature, your heater shuts off. Similarly, your body has mechanisms in place that help you to maintain a constant body temperature of about 37 degrees Celsius. If your internal temperature rises as a result of exercise or exertion, your body responds by sweating. The evaporation of moisture from your skin cools your body and brings it back into an acceptable temperature range. Many hormones, such as **insulin,** act through negative-feedback mechanisms.

REVIEW FOR LESSON 6

Take a few moments to practice test-taking strategies for questions about the similarities and differences in living things. The answers and explanations are on page 74.

1 The absorption and circulation of materials in a hydra are most similar to the absorption and circulation of materials in a(n)—

A frog

B earthworm

C *Amoeba*

D grasshopper

2 Which statement correctly describes one characteristic of the digestive system of a grasshopper?

F The shape of the system allows food to be processed by intracellular digestion.

G Various parts of the system perform different digestive functions.

H The system is characterized by a single opening through which food enters and waste exits.

J Food is phagocytized at the surface of the grasshopper.

3 Which title is an appropriate heading for column *X*?

Organism	X
A	plasma membrane
B	Malpighian tubules
C	nephridia

A Structures Needed for Anaerobic Respiration

B Structures Used in Gas Exchange

C Excretory Systems

D Sensory Receptors

4 Which environmental cue affects seasonal patterns of behavior in plants and animals?

F Changes in moisture availability

G Changes in temperature

H Changes in duration of sunlight

J Changes in air pressure

5 Plants bend toward the light because cells on the dark side of the stem elongate. Cell elongation is influenced by hormones known as—

A auxins

B adenines

C ethylene gas

D gibberellins

ANSWERS AND EXPLANATIONS

1 **C** *Amoeba.* **A, B,** and **D** are large, multicellular organisms with specific organ systems for both life functions.

2 **G Various parts of the system perform different digestive functions.** Animals are characterized by an internal body cavity that performs extracellular digestion not intracellular, so **F** is incorrect. **H** is incorrect because a grasshopper has two openings, a mouth for ingestion and an anus for excretion. **J** is wrong because phagocytosis, known as cell-eating, is used by unicellular organisms.

3 **C Excretory Systems. A** does not make sense. **B** would include lungs, moist skin, gills, and so forth. **D** would include skin, antennae, whiskers, and so forth.

4 **H Changes in duration of sunlight.** Changes in moisture availability, **F,** may have a short-term impact, but does not generally influence long-term behavior. Changes in temperature, **G,** are the result of changes in duration of sunlight. Changes in air pressure, **J,** do not generally influence long-term behavior patterns.

5 **A auxins.** These are hormones that regulate cell growth, causing the appearance of phototropism in plants. **B** is a nitrogenous base, **C** is a hormone-like gas that influences fruit-ripening and fruit drop, and **D** is a hormone that promotes stem elongation and seed germination.

LESSON 7

HUMANS

Until now, you've seen that the human body shares many structural and functional characteristics with other animals. Of course, human beings are unique in their own right. (Have you ever seen an earthworm dance?) So, now the question becomes, "What makes humans so special?"

STRUCTURE, SUPPORT, AND LOCOMOTION

What makes humans unique among all the organisms on Earth is that humans are the only ones that walk upright. The fact that humans have an upright orientation is made possible by the structure of the human **endoskeleton** (an internal supporting skeleton). The endoskeleton gives the body its distinctively human shape and support for muscle attachments. The combination of muscles and bones produces the characteristic human modes of locomotion—walking and running. In several ways, locomotion is a life function that gives heterotrophic organisms, i.e., humans, an edge over autotrophic organisms. The ability to move allows humans to accomplish the following:

- find food
- find suitable habitats
- find mates
- flee from predators

THE SKELETAL SYSTEM

The human skeletal system is made up of specialized tissues—**bones**, **cartilage**, and **ligaments**—that provide a strong framework against which muscles can pull. Joints, places where bones meet, allow for a wider range of movement and flexibility than would otherwise be possible. Located deep within the bones is bone marrow, which is the site of red blood cell production.

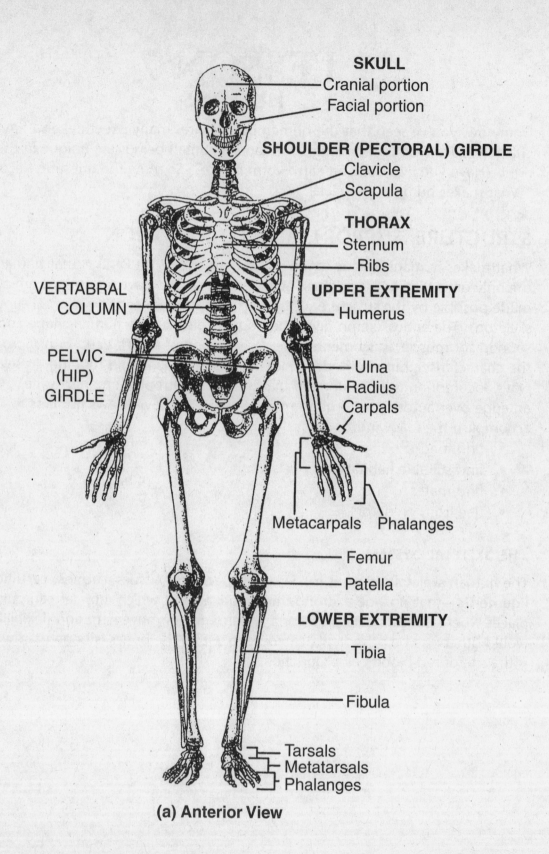

SKULL
Cranial portion
Facial portion

SHOULDER (PECTORAL) GIRDLE
Clavicle
Scapula

THORAX
Sternum
Ribs

UPPER EXTREMITY
Humerus
Ulna
Radius
Carpals

VERTABRAL COLUMN

PELVIC (HIP) GIRDLE

Metacarpals   Phalanges

Femur
Patella

LOWER EXTREMITY
Tibia

Fibula

Tarsals
Metatarsals
Phalanges

(a) Anterior View

Muscle Systems

There are three types of muscles that operate in the human body: **smooth, cardiac,** and **skeletal.** Smooth and cardiac muscles are responsible for *involuntary* movements, while skeletal muscles are responsible for *voluntary* movements. Because muscle fibers can only contract, pairs of muscles are usually needed to move a joint. **Flexors** are muscles that cause limbs to bend at joints. Biceps and hamstrings are two examples. **Extensors** are muscles that extend joints, causing limbs to straighten. Flexor and extensor muscles are attached to bones by **tendons. Ligaments** are tissues that connect one bone to another. Together, muscles and bones act as simple machines called levers.

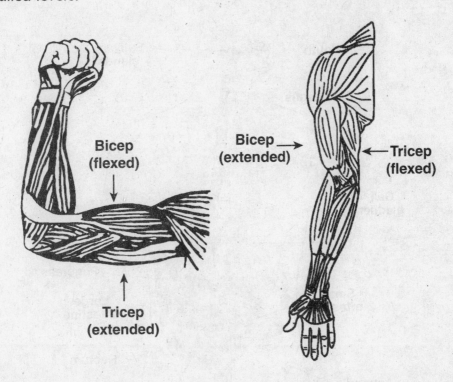

Bicep
(flexed)

Tricep
(extended)

Bicep
(extended)

Tricep
(flexed)

NUTRITION

As part of a proper diet, you need to eat a balance of carbohydrates, fats, proteins, vitamins, and minerals. The digestive system is a system of organs and tissues designed to break down food into its macromolecular components—carbohydrates, fats, and proteins—which are then absorbed by the bloodstream and fed into the cells.

THE DIGESTIVE SYSTEM

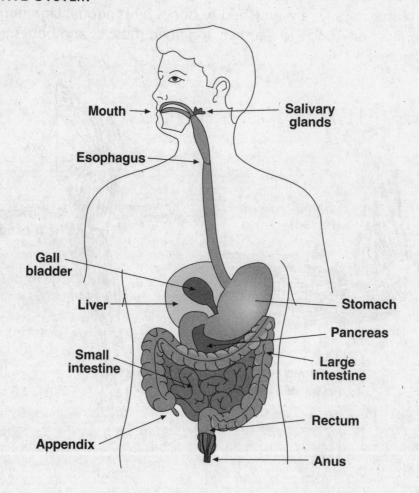

The mouth

The first stop in the digestive process is the mouth, or **oral cavity.** Your teeth break up large food particles into smaller pieces that mix with **saliva.** Saliva contains the enzyme salivary amylase, which starts the breakdown of carbohydrates. The food then passes from the mouth to the stomach through the **esophagus.** Food is pushed through the esophagus by wavelike muscular contractions known as **peristalsis.**

The stomach

The next stop is the stomach. The stomach is a thick, muscular sack that has the following three main functions:

- It temporarily stores ingested food.
- It partially digests protein.
- It kills bacteria.

The stomach secretes gastric juices that contain digestive enzymes and hydrochloric acid (HCl). One of the most important digestive enzymes is **pepsin.** Pepsin breaks down proteins by splitting the bonds between the amino acids. When HCl is secreted by the lining of the stomach, the pH of the stomach is lowered, which activates pepsin. The lining of the stomach is also covered by a thick coat of mucus that protects the structural tissue from its own acidic secretions. Last but not least, HCl kills bacteria found in ingested foods.

Once food is broken down into a blob of partially digested material and enzymes, or **chyme,** it leaves the stomach and enters the small intestine. This is where the most of the digestion takes place.

The small intestine

The small intestine might seem like a silly name for this part of the body. After all, an average man's small intestine is a whooping twenty-three feet long! However, this organ earned its name not from its length, but from its width: The small intestine is only about an inch in diameter. Once in the small intestine, carbohydrates, proteins, and fats are broken down into sugars, amino acids, glycerol, and fatty acids. These substances are absorbed into the bloodstream through the walls of the small intestine. Within these walls are tiny, fingerlike projections called **villi,** which increase the surface area available for absorption, and therefore the amount of nutrients absorbed. The unabsorbed and undigested materials leave the small intestine and enter the **large intestine (colon)** for the last stop of the digestion process.

The large intestine

The last opportunity for absorption in the digestive system is the large intestine. This intestine is much shorter than the small intestine (it's about three feet long), but it is thicker than its counterpart. The large intestine absorbs any leftover water and minerals from undigested material that leaves the small intestine. The concentrated solid moves into the rectum and passes out of the body through the anus.

EXCRETORY SYSTEM

The excretory system removes metabolic wastes from humans. **Kidneys** play a critical role in the removal of nitrogenous wastes from the blood and the maintenance of water and ion concentrations. Think of the kidneys as a pair of filters that remove any unwanted materials from your body. They process blood as it passes through its structures and eventually send the liquid waste to the **bladder** through the **ureters**. Liquid waste is stored in the bladder until it is eliminated from the body through the **urethra**.

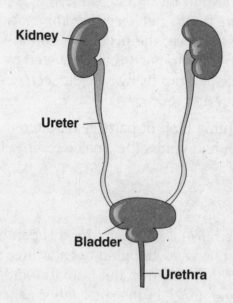

OTHER EXCRETORY ORGANS

Lungs

Lungs function in the removal of carbon dioxide, water vapor, and the products of cellular respiration.

Liver

The liver functions in the removal of damaged or old red blood cells from the body. It also produces **urea**, which is formed as the result of the breakdown of amino acids.

Skin

You probably never thought of your skin as an excretory organ, but the skin actively removes wastes from the body. How? The **sweat glands** in your skin remove water, salts, and urea from the body, which are secreted as your everyday sweat or **perspiration**.

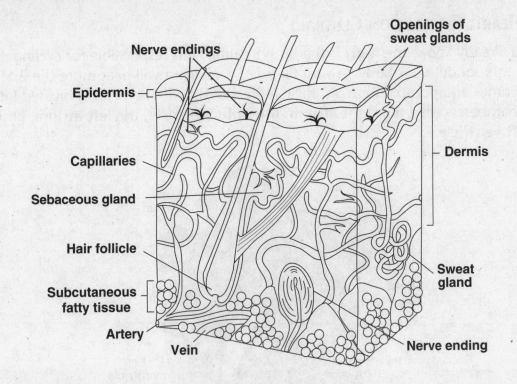

Labels on the diagram:
- Nerve endings
- Epidermis
- Capillaries
- Sebaceous gland
- Hair follicle
- Subcutaneous fatty tissue
- Artery
- Vein
- Openings of sweat glands
- Dermis
- Sweat gland
- Nerve ending

TRANSPORT

So far, you've read about how humans eat, digest, and excrete wastes. But what about the nutrients? How do they get to where they are going?

THE CIRCULATORY SYSTEM

Until **William Harvey** discovered how blood circulates in 1616, the movement of materials inside the body was a mystery. It is now known that the circulatory system is made of a series of transport structures that conduct a specialized tissue, **blood,** from one place to another. The tissue known as blood is actually a mixture of red blood cells (or corpuscles), platelets, white blood cells, and plasma. The circulatory system also plays a role in homeostasis, as it provides humans with a method of transferring heat from one part of the body to another.

THE HEART: CIRCULATION CENTRAL

As you already know, the heart is the body's pump. It is responsible for cycling blood throughout your body. In your lifetime, your heart will beat more the 2.5 billion times and pump about 180 million liters of blood! The heart is divided into four chambers, called the **right atrium**, the **right ventricle**, the **left atrium**, and the **left ventricle**.

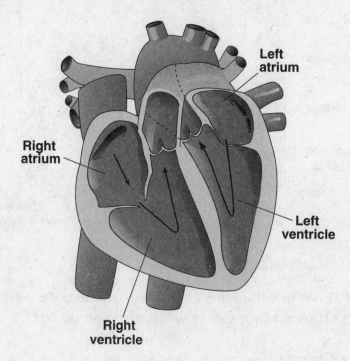

As you can tell from the arrows, the heart pumps blood in a continuous circuit. Blood flows in from the lungs into the left atrium, to the left ventricle, and then out of the aorta toward the rest of the body. It then returns to the right atrium, flows into the right ventricle, and goes back to the lungs via the pulmonary arteries.

Before moving on, take a look at the point at which the blood exits the left ventricle. When blood leaves the left ventricle, it starts its long tour of the body. This tour is called the **systemic circulation**.

Systemic circulation

Blood leaves the heart through a large blood vessel called the **aorta**, which is the largest artery in the body. It carries blood away from the heart. Just remember, **A**rteries carry blood **A**way from the heart. Arteries are thick-walled, but elastic vessels. Their strength and elasticity make it possible for them to manage the high-pressure flow of blood being pumped away from the heart.

The arteries branch into smaller vessels called arterioles, and finally into the smallest vessels, the capillaries, which are tiny tubes only one cell thick. In fact, blood cells must pass through the capillaries single file.

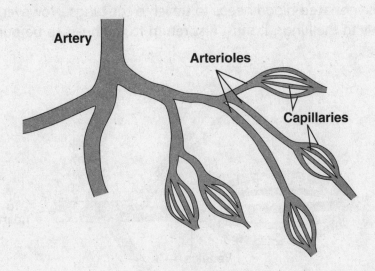

There are thousands and thousands of capillaries in the body. In fact, it is estimated that the capillary routes in your bloodstream total as much one hundred kilometers, which is roughly the distance from Richmond to Charlottesville! Capillaries intermingle with the body's tissues, facilitating the exchange of nutrients, gases, and wastes.

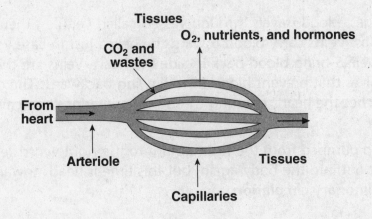

Back to the heart

After touring the body, the blood has very little oxygen left—most of its oxygen has passed through capillary walls into the body's cells. In order to get a fresh supply of oxygen, the **deoxygenated** blood needs to travel to the lungs. However, the blood doesn't go directly to the lungs. It must first return to the heart to be pumped out again.

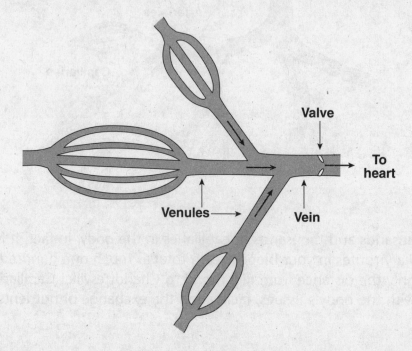

From the capillaries, blood travels through vessels called venules, then into larger vessels called veins. **Veins** carry blood toward the heart. Just in case you forget, remember that ve**INS** bring blood back **INS**ide the heart. Veins are thin-walled vessels with one-way valves that prevent blood from flowing backward. The deoxygenated blood finally reaches the heart, entering through the inferior **vena cava** and into the right atrium.

The blood is then pumped from the right atrium to the right ventricle. From there, the blood travels out into the body again, but this time it heads toward the lungs in what's called **pulmonary circulation.**

Pulmonary circulation

Blood leaves the right ventricle through a large artery known as the **pulmonary artery.** The pulmonary artery branches into the right and left pulmonary arteries, which lead to the lungs. These arteries then branch into arterioles, and finally into capillaries. The capillaries in the lungs are wrapped around **alveoli,** which are tiny air sacs.

While at the alveoli, blood picks up the oxygen that the body needs. At this point, the **oxygenated** blood returns to the heart via the **pulmonary veins** and enters the left atrium.

The diagram below maps out the flow of blood into, through, and out of the heart. The numbers **1, 2, 3,** and **4** indicate the path that blood follows through the heart.

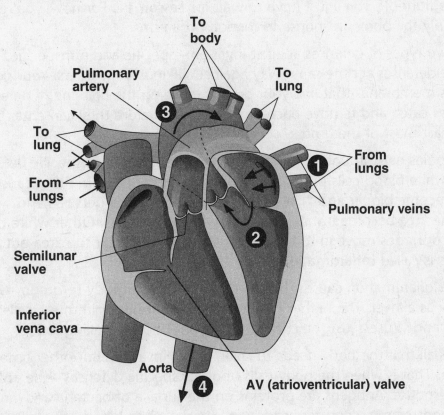

Once the blood moves to the left ventricle, it's ready to start the entire process again.

LYMPH: THE *OTHER* CIRCULATORY SYSTEM

The lymphatic system is a secondary system that cycles blood plasma, or **lymph.** Lymph is circulated through the body using the standard arterial system. However, on its way back to the heart, it does not use the venous system. Instead, while deoxygenated blood containing carbon dioxide and other substances enters the venous system through the venous capillaries, lymph is separated and directed into the lymphatic capillaries where it enters the lymphatic system. On its way back to the heart, wastes and cellular debris are filtered out of the lymph and into lymph nodes, which are located at specific points along the way. The lymph system plays a significant role in the body's immune response.

THE IMMUNE RESPONSE

So, you may wonder, how does your body win the war against invaders? The immune response is your body's way of attacking and removing a foreign substance. It could be bacteria, a virus, a cancer cell, or a transplanted organ—all the body knows is that it doesn't belong. If you're worried about what kind of invaders the body has to fight off, you'll just have to wait for Lesson 11. For now, you're going to review only the body's response to foreign organisms.

You have two types of defenses against invasion—specific and nonspecific. Nonspecific defenses act the same way against all kinds of invaders. Your skin and the mucous membranes that line your organs make up the first line of defense. These tissues catch and remove bacteria and viruses before they can enter the body—at least most of the time.

If foreign bodies get through the first line, then the second nonspecific defense kicks in. Special white blood cells produce a chemical called **histamine** that causes blood vessels to become bigger and "leakier." As a result, the area gets red and swells. The nerves in the area become irritated and the whole part hurts. Other white blood cells called **macrophages** move in to engulf the invaders and clear the area out. This process is called **inflammation.**

Sometimes, inflammation causes the temperature of your body to go up—what you better know as a fever. The higher temperatures are good for immune cells and bad for bacteria and viruses. Just the combination your body is looking for.

Often this is all that the body needs to clean up an invasion. But other times, it is not enough. That is when the body calls upon its specific defenses—the **antigen-antibody** response. Antigens are proteins on the surface of bacteria and viruses that the bloodstream recognizes as foreign. Special white blood cells called **B-lymphocytes** produce a chemical called an antibody that binds to those molecules and disables the cell or virus. The antibody also attracts a special white blood cell called a **T-lymphocyte,** which uses phagocytosis (cell-eating) to engulf and digest the disabled bacteria.

This is known as a primary response, and it takes time. But once your body learns to recognize and defend against a specific invader—it remembers. Special cells continue to circulate for the rest of your life that can immediately spring into action when exposed to that exact invader again. That's why once you get the measles, you are immune to them in the futurte. Unfortunately, this doesn't work well with viruses because they mutate so quickly. It is almost impossible to get exactly the same virus twice. Doctors can expose you to deadly bacteria in tiny weakened doses, just enough so you can learn to recognize the bacteria, but not so much that it hurts you. These shots are called **vaccines.**

RESPIRATION

Go back and take a closer look at the organs in the respiratory system and how they function in supplying cells with oxygen. In order for cellular respiration to take place in aerobic organisms, molecular oxygen is needed. The respiratory system plays a vital role in providing the oxygen needed to carry out cellular respiration.

The respiratory system

The human respiratory system is composed of several interrelated structures that function together for the purpose of gas exchange.

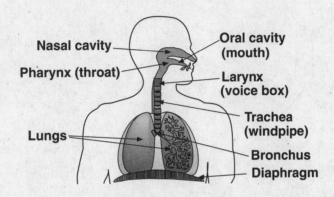

Air enters the respiratory system through the **nasal cavity,** which is lined with hair and ciliated cells that filter out dust particles. From the nasal cavity, air is drawn into the **pharynx** at the back of the nasal cavity, and past the **epiglottis** that covers the trachea to prevent food from entering it. The **trachea** (windpipe) is a tube-shaped structure that connects the pharynx to two **bronchi.** Both the trachea and bronchi are lined with ciliated tissues that filter out particulate matter before the air enters the lungs. As the bronchi enter lung tissue, they branch into progressively smaller structures called **bronchioles** until they finally terminate at tiny air sacs called **alveoli,** which are surrounded by capillaries. Oxygen diffuses into the blood flowing through the capillaries. It is then transported back to the heart and circulated throughout the body. The oxygen is then delivered to different tissues and organs, where the blood picks up carbon dioxide. Carbon dioxide returns to the lungs, where it diffuses out of the blood in the capillaries and into the alveoli. It then moves through the respiratory system and exits the body.

Take a deep breath

The act of respiring is the result of the joint effort between the **diaphragm**—a muscular structure that separates the chest cavity from the abdominal cavity—and the muscles that surround the rib cage. Remember that in diffusion, substances move from areas of high concentration to areas of low concentration. The same holds true for the movement of air. If the air pressure inside your lungs is higher than the air pressure outside of your lungs, air moves out of your lungs (you exhale). If the air pressure outside of your lungs is higher than the air pressure inside your lungs, air moves into your lungs (you inhale). The actions of the diaphragm and chest muscles around your rib cage control the pressure conditions inside your lungs.

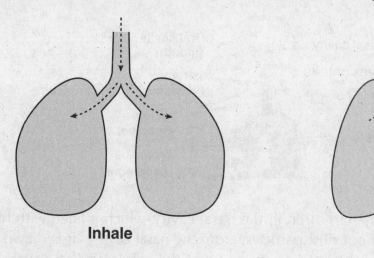

Inhale   **Exhale**

REGULATION

All organisms must be able to react to changes in their environments. As a result, organisms have evolved systems that enable them to pick up cues from the outside world. The task of coordinating and processing this information falls to the nervous system (nerve control) and endocrine system (chemical control).

THE NERVOUS SYSTEM

The basic unit of structure and function in the nervous system is a **neuron.**
Neurons are specialized cells that pick up and transmit messages throughout
the body. Neurons consist of a **cyton** (the cell body), **dendrites,** and an **axon.**

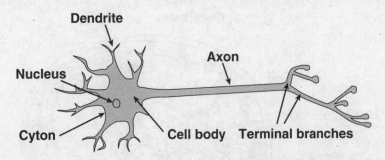

The cyton contains the nucleus and all the usual organelles found in the cytoplasm.
The dendrites are short extensions of the cell body that receive the stimuli. The axon
is a long, slender extension of the cell body that transmits an impulse from the cell
body to another neuron. At the end of the axon are thin fibers known as terminal
branches. These branches release **neurotransmitters.** Neurotransmitters enable
messages to be passed from one neuron to another.

When a message arrives at a dendrite, it passes into the cell body, then down the
axon to the terminal branches. When an impulse reaches the end of the axon, it
triggers the release of a neurotransmitter into the space between the first cell's axon
and the next cell's dendrites. This space is called a **synapse.** The neurotransmitter
"swims" to the other side and binds to receptors on the dendrites of the next
neuron. Now, the impulse moves along the second neuron, from dendrites to axon.
It's the neurotransmitter that triggers the passing of the signal to the second neuron.

As you might expect, the human nervous system is a complicated series of neurons.
There are literally billions of neurons running throughout your body. The nervous
system of humans and many animals can be divided into two parts: the **central
nervous system** and the **peripheral nervous system.**

The Central Nervous System

The central nervous system includes the brain and the spinal cord. The brain is a large, jellylike organ made mostly of water and fat. It's divided into three regions, each of which is associated with a specific type of function.

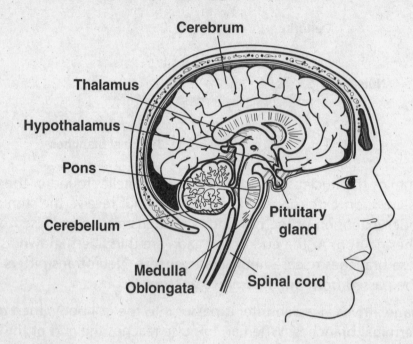

Regions of the brain

Cerebellum: helps coordinate motor control and equilibrium.

Cerebrum: center of sensory-motor coordination; regulates conscious thought, speech, and judgment; site of memory, intelligence, and personality.

Hypothalamus: regulates blood pressure, body temperature, and heart rate; controls basic human behaviors, such as eating, drinking, and sleeping.

Medulla oblongata: helps control heart rate, respiration, and gastrointestinal functions.

Pituitary gland: produces hormones that activate other glands and responds to negative feedback mechanisms.

Pons: relays information from the medulla oblongata to higher brain centers, linking parts of the brain to each other.

The spinal cord

The spinal cord is actually an extension of the brain. It connects the brain to the peripheral nerves and coordinates reflex responses. The bony vertebral column as well as the cerebrospinal fluid protect the spinal cord from injury.

THE PERIPHERAL NERVOUS SYSTEM

The peripheral nervous system is composed of sensory and motor neurons. It can be divided into two systems: **autonomic** and **somatic.** The autonomic nervous system includes nerves that regulate responses associated with involuntary tissues, such as smooth and cardiac muscle. The somatic nervous system governs the actions of voluntary tissues, such as skeletal muscles.

THE ENDOCRINE SYSTEM: IN IT FOR THE LONG HAUL

Neurotransmitters produced by the nervous system provide short-term solutions in situations requiring regulation. For the long haul, the human body pulls out its trump card: hormones. The endocrine system is composed of glands located at various locations throughout the body that secrete hormones. The **pituitary gland,** located in the brain, is the master of all glands. The **thyroid gland,** located in the neck, produces thyroxine, a hormone that regulates the metabolic rates of cells. **Parathyroid glands** produce parathyroid hormone, which regulates blood calcium levels. The **islets of Langerhans** secrete the hormone insulin. Insulin directs the storage of glucose in the liver in the form of **glycogen.**

REVIEW FOR LESSON 7

Take a few moments to practice test-taking strategies for questions about human physiology. The answers and explanations are on page 94.

1 In some regions of the world, children suffer from a protein deficiency known as kwashiorkor. This deficiency occurs when a child's diet is changed from high-protein breast milk to watery cereal. Although the child is receiving calories, the child becomes sick and less active, and growth ceases. These symptoms are probably due to—

A too much saturated fat in the diet

B an overconsumption of high-protein foods

C not enough carbohydrates in the diet

D insufficient essential amino acids in the diet

2 Which endocrine gland secretes a hormone that accelerates metabolic activities in times of emergency?

F Thyroid

G Adrenal

H Pancreas

J Parathyroid

3 Which chamber of the human heart sends blood to the lungs?

A Left ventricle

B Right ventricle

C Left atrium

D Right atrium

4 Which compounds are produced in human muscle cells as a result of the oxidation of glucose in the absence of oxygen?

F Amino acids and water

G Lactic acid and ATP

H Oxygen and methane

J Ethyl alcohol and ATP

5 In the human elbow joint, the bone of the upper arm is connected to the bones of the lower arm by flexible connective tissues known as—

A muscles

B neurons

C tendons

D ligaments

ANSWERS AND EXPLANATIONS

1 **D insufficient essential amino acids in the diet. A, B,** and **C** do not cause the protein deficiency associated with kwashiorkor.

2 **G Adrenal.** This is a straight memorization question, but you could look at the question for clues and try a little word association using key words, such as "emergency" and "accelerating." Adrenaline is the flight-or-fight hormone produced by the adrenal gland. **F,** thyroid, produces thyroxine, which regulates growth. **H** is an organ, not a gland, although it does contain a gland that produces insulin. **J** produces parathyroid hormone.

3 **B Right ventricle. A,** left ventricle, pumps oxygenated blood to the body. **C,** left atrium, receives oxygenated blood from the lungs. **D,** right atrium, receives deoxygenated blood from the body.

4 **G Lactic acid and ATP.** Here you are looking for the products produced during cellular respiration without oxygen present. If oxygen were present, it would be an aerobic process. However, in this case, you are dealing with anaerobic cellular respiration in human muscle cells. ATP is produced during cellular respiration. Under anaerobic conditions, human muscle cells carry out lactic acid fermentation. Alcohol fermentation results in the production of ethyl alcohol and ATP, **J. F** and **H** are not reasonable choices.

5 **D ligaments. A** and **B** are important for bone movement, but do not connect bones. **C** connects muscle to bone.

LESSON 8
CELL REPRODUCTION
AND HUMAN REPRODUCTION

Reproduction refers to the ability of living things to grow and produce offspring. In this lesson, you will take a look at both asexual and sexual reproduction. Because reproduction begins on a cellular level, let's start with the **somatic** (body) cell.

THE CELL CYCLE

The cells of all living things grow and multiply through a cycle made up of four phases. During the first three of these phases (G_1, S, and G_2 of interphase), the cell is growing and metabolically active. During the fourth phase, it is undergoing division to produce two new cells (mitosis). The amount of time the cell spends in the cycle depends on its type; for instance, some cells in the body take about 15 hours to go through a complete cycle, whereas for cells in your brain, the cycle can take years. Take a look at the diagram below depicting the cycle of a typical cell.

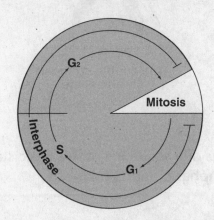

MITOSIS

Every second, thousands of cells are reproducing throughout your body. Somatic cells are able to make identical copies of themselves at an amazing rate, thanks to a means of asexual reproduction known as **mitosis.**

You need to be familiar with the process of mitosis for the EOC Biology exam. During mitosis, two things occur: the cell duplicates its genetic material and the cell splits in half, forming two daughter cells, both of which are identical to the parent cell. The process of mitosis begins when the chromosomes in the nucleus duplicate themselves.

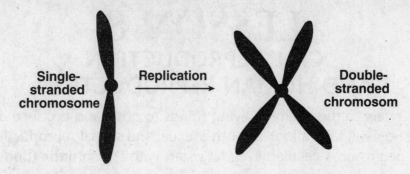

Single-stranded chromosome → Replication → Double-stranded chromosom

The original chromosome and its new twin are linked, as you can see in the figure below. These identical chromosomes are now called **sister chromatids**. The chromatids are held together by a round structure called the **centromere**.

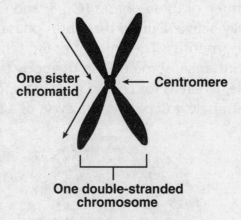

One sister chromatid — Centromere

One double-stranded chromosome

THE STAGES OF MITOSIS

In a nutshell, mitosis consists of a sequence of five basic stages: **prophase, metaphase, anaphase, telophase,** and **cytokinesis.**

Prophase

In prophase, the newly replicated chromosomes condense and become visible. One of the first signs of prophase is the disintegration of the nuclear membrane. During prophase, paired structures called the **centrioles** (see Lesson 5) start to move away from each other toward opposite ends of the cell. The centrioles spin out a system of microtubules known as the spindle fibers, which grow toward the chromosomes.

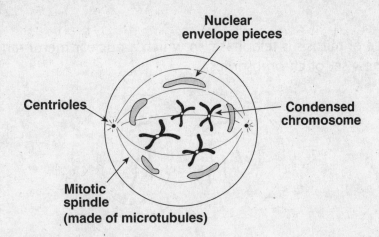

Nuclear
envelope pieces

Centrioles

Condensed
chromosome

Mitotic
spindle
(made of microtubules)

Metaphase

The next stage in mitosis is called metaphase. In metaphase, the chromosomes begin to line up along the equator of the cell. Notice how nice and orderly they've become.

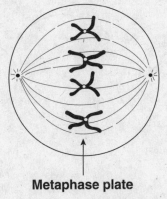

Metaphase plate

The spindle fibers are responsible for this neat arrangement. They help align the chromosomes at the middle of the cell along its equator, also known as the **metaphase plate**.

Anaphase

During anaphase, the sister chromatids of each chromosome separate at the centromere and slowly move to opposite poles. An apparent tug-of-war takes place as the spindle fibers pull the chromosomes apart and drag them to opposite ends of the cell.

Telophase

The next phase of mitosis is telophase, in which a nuclear membrane begins to form around each new set of chromosomes.

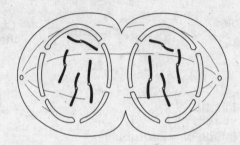

Cytokinesis

Now it's time to split the cytoplasm in cytokinesis. Look at the figure below and you'll notice that the cell membrane has begun to split along a **cleavage furrow.**

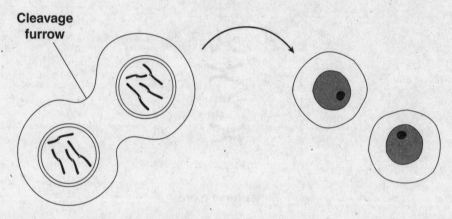

A cell membrane forms around each cell, which are split into two new daughter cells. This is the final stage of mitosis.

You've read how cytokinesis occurs in animal cells, but in plant cells, this final phase is slightly different. Plant cells do not form cleavage furrows. Instead, a partition called a cell plate forms down the middle region, separating the two daughter cells. In addition to this difference, plant cells do not contain centrioles. Otherwise, mitosis is pretty much the same in plant and animal cells.

Mnemonic for mitosis

If you need a little help remembering the stages of mitosis, try using the following mnemonic to help you out:

PMATC	
Prophase . . .	**P** is for **P**repare (as the cell prepares for mitosis)
Metaphase . . .	**M** is for **M**eet (when the chromosomes meet in the middle)
Anaphase . . .	**A** is for **A**part (when the chromosomes draw apart)
Telophase . . .	**T** is for **T**ake over (as a nuclear membrane begins to form and take over each new set of chromosomes)
Cytokinesis . . .	**C** is for **C**ut (as the cell is cut in half, forming two daughter cells)

What's the purpose of asexual reproduction?

The purpose of asexual reproduction is to create daughter cells that are identical copies of the single parent cell. In animal cells, all cells except sex cells undergo mitosis.

BINARY FISSION

Prokaryotic cells, such as bacteria, undergo a form of asexual reproduction called **binary fission.** Binary fission is just like mitosis; bacteria replicate their chromosomes and divide into two identical daughter cells. This method of asexual reproduction is also common in *Paramecium* and *Amoeba*.

BUDDING

Other organisms, such as yeast and hydra, reproduce asexually by budding. Budding is a process in which little buds sprout from the parent and eventually develop into a fully formed offspring. As you can see from the following graphic, the cell divides unequally:

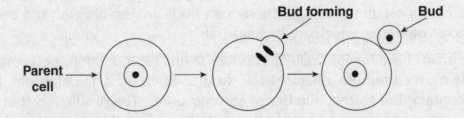

SPORULATION

Another form of asexual reproduction is sporulation. Fungi, for example, produce **spores** (airborne cells) that are released from the parent organism into the air.

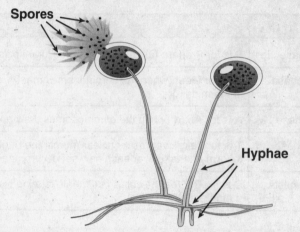

Once these tiny haploid cells land on fertile ground, they reproduce mitotically, generating other fungi. *Rhizopus*, a common bread mold, reproduces asexually by sporulation.

MEIOSIS

Every organism has a specific number of chromosomes. For example, fruit flies have eight chromosomes; humans have forty-six chromosomes. However, if you take a closer look at a human cell, you'll realize that humans actually possess only twenty-three different chromosomes.

So, why do humans have two of each? In normal eukaryotic cells, chromosomes exist in pairs called **homologues.** When a cell has a full complement of homologues, or homologous chromosomes as they're often called, it is said to be a **diploid.** A normal diploid human cell contains forty-six chromosomes altogether, two of each kind. Therefore, the **diploid number** for humans is forty-six. Some cells possess only *one* set of chromosomes, and they are called **haploid.** For instance, a haploid human cell contains a total of twenty-three chromosomes.

The terms diploid and haploid are important when you learn about sexual reproduction. Almost all the cells in the human body are diploid with the exception of sex cells, or **gametes,** which are haploid cells.

Why do humans have haploid cells? In human sexual reproduction, both the male and female must contribute a haploid cell, so that when their gametes join, the offspring contains the correct number of chromosomes. The problem is that each of them has a full set of chromosomes in their regular cells. If they both threw in their full complement, the baby would have forty-six pairs instead of twenty-three. Within a few generations, babies would be born with 1,507,328 pairs of chromosomes! To preserve the diploid number of chromosomes in an organism, each parent must contribute only half of his or her chromosomes. **Meiosis** is the process by which sexually reproducing organisms maintain the same number of chromosomes from generation to generation.

Because sexually reproducing organisms require haploid cells only for reproduction, meiosis is limited to sex cells in special sex organs called **gonads.** The gonads in males are the **testes,** and in females, they are the **ovaries.**

THE STAGES OF MEIOSIS

Meiosis involves two rounds of cell division: the **first meiotic division** and **second meiotic division.** As in mitosis, the chromosomes duplicate and double-stranded chromosomes are formed in interphase of the cell cycle, before cell division begins.

The first meiotic division

Meiosis I consists of four stages: **prophase I, metaphase I, anaphase I,** and **telophase I.**

Prophase I chromosomes

Prophase I is a little more complicated than mitotic prophase. As in mitosis, the nuclear membrane begins to disappear, the chromosomes become visible, and the centrioles move to opposite poles of the nucleus. But that's where the similarity ends.

In prophase I, the chromosomes line up side by side with their counterparts, in an event known as **synapsis.**

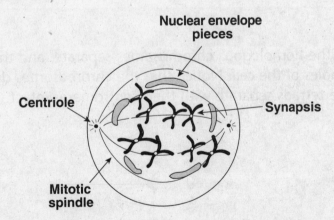

Synapsis involves two sets of chromosomes coming together to form a **tetrad.** A tetrad consists of four chromatids. Synapsis is followed by crossing-over, which is the exchange of segments of homologous chromosomes.

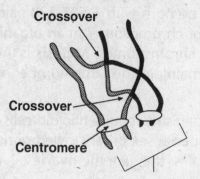

Crossover

Crossover

Centromere

Homologous chromosomes

What's unique in prophase I is that pieces of homologous chromosomes are swapped between the partners in the tetrad. This is one of the ways organisms produce genetic variation.

Metaphase I

As is the case in mitosis, the chromosome pairs—the tetrads—line up at the metaphase plate in metaphase I.

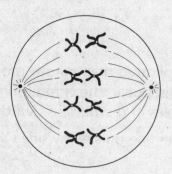

Anaphase I

During anaphase I, the homologous chromosomes separate, and the chromosomes move to opposite poles of the cell. Notice that the chromosomes do not separate at the centromere; the tetrads separate with their centromeres intact.

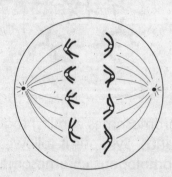

Telophase I

During telophase I, a nuclear membrane begins to form around each set of chromosomes.

The cells finally undergo cytokinesis, yielding two daughter cells.

The second meiotic division

The second meiotic division is virtually identical to mitosis. After a brief period, the cell undergoes a second round of cell division. During **prophase II**, the chromosomes once again condense. In **metaphase II**, the chromosomes move toward the metaphase plate. During **anaphase II**, the chromatids of each chromosome split at the centromere and move to opposite ends of the cell. During **telophase II**, a new nuclear membrane envelope begins to form around each set of chromosomes. Four new daughter cells are produced at the end of the second round of meiosis.

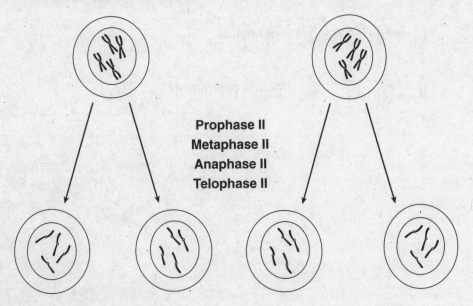

Prophase II
Metaphase II
Anaphase II
Telophase II

The resulting cells, each of which contains only half the total number of chromosomes, are haploid gametes.

Gametogenesis

Because meiosis results in the formation of gametes, it is also known as **gametogenesis.** When meiosis takes place in the male gonads, it results in the production of sperm cells. This is called **spermatogenesis.** During spermatogenesis, four sperm cells are produced from each parent cell.

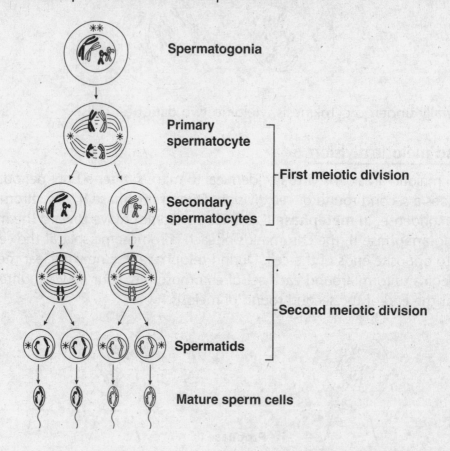

In a female, an egg cell, or ovum, is produced as the result of meiosis. This process is called **oogenesis.** Oogenesis differs slightly from spermatogenensis in that only one ovum is produced.

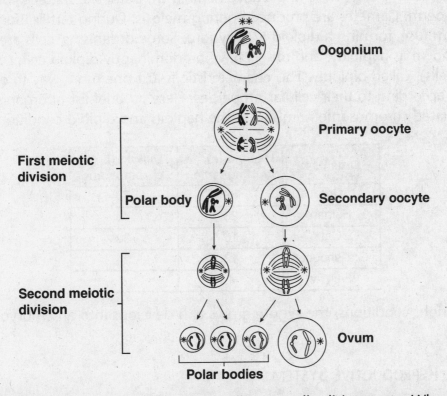

The other three cells, called polar bodies, will eventually disintegrate. Why do women produce only one ovum? Well, because the female wants to conserve as much cytoplasm as possible to nurture the surviving gamete. This means that the ovum contains a lot of stored nutrients.

Here's a summary of the major differences between mitosis and meiosis.

MITOSIS	MEIOSIS
Occurs in somatic (body) cells	Occurs in germ (sex) cells
Produces identical cells	Produces gametes
Diploid cells → diploid cells	Diploid cells → haploid cells

THE HUMAN REPRODUCTIVE SYSTEM

For sexually reproducing species, such as humans, the goal of both the male and female reproductive systems is to produce haploid (*n*) gametes, better known as eggs and sperm. Gametes are produced during meiosis. During fertilization, an egg and a sperm fuse, forming a diploid (2*n*) zygote. Some organisms' cells are always haploid, known as haploidy, and others have predominantly diploid cells (except for germ cells), called diploidy. This characteristic is just one more way to categorize organisms according to their cellular properties. Here's a brief list of organisms and their associated chromosome numbers in the haploid and diploid condition.

Organism	Haploid (*n*) chromosomes	Diploid (2*n*) chromosome
Dog	39	78
Human	23	46
Cat	16	32
Grasshopper	12	24
Fruit fly	4	8

Under the right conditions, the zygote grows and develops into an embryo and then into a fetus.

THE MALE REPRODUCTIVE SYSTEM

The male reproductive system functions in the production and delivery of male gametes (sperm cells). During **spermatogenesis,** sperm are produced by meiosis and stored in the **testes.** The testes are also the sites of testosterone production. At the time of activation, sperm move through a system of tubes and are mixed with fluids secreted by glands. This mixture of fluids and sperm, now called **semen,** exits the body through the **urethra** and out through the penis. The penis is a structural adaptation that permits internal fertilizaton.

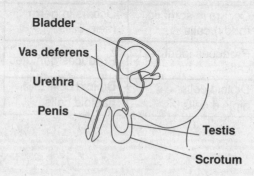

THE FEMALE REPRODUCTIVE SYSTEM

In women, the ovaries are responsible for the production of the female gametes (egg cells). Ovaries also act as endocrine glands; they release hormones that play crucial roles in reproduction. The main roles of the ovaries are the following:

- to manufacture **ova**
- to secrete **estrogen** and **progesterone**, the principal female sex hormones

Whereas males produce sperm throughout their lives, females are born with more than two million immature egg cells stored in the **follicles** of each ovary. At sexual maturity, the ovaries prepare and release mature ovum (eggs) in a series of events called the **ovarian**, or **menstrual**, **cycle**.

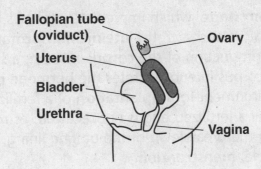

Fallopian tube (oviduct)

Ovary

Uterus

Bladder

Urethra

Vagina

The menstrual cycle

The menstrual cycle takes place in a series of hormone-regulated stages over the course of an average twenty-eight-day cycle. The pituitary gland signals the start of the follicle stage by inducing the production of **follicle stimulating hormone (FSH)**. During this stage, FSH stimulates an egg to mature within the ovary. The follicle stage lasts approximately fourteen days and ends at **ovulation**. Additionally, FSH production initiates estrogen production. Estrogen signals the lining of the uterus to thicken and grow blood vessels (vascularize). During ovulation, a mature ova is released from the follicle into the **oviduct (fallopian tube)**—a short tube that leads from the follicle to the **uterus**, where **fertilization** may take place if sperm are present.

During the **corpus luteum stage**, which immediately follows the follicle stage and ovulation, the pituitary gland secretes **luteinizing hormone (LH)**. Luteinizing hormone stimulates the production of the **corpus luteum**, a structure formed from the ovarian follicle. The corpus luteum secretes the hormone **progesterone**, which prapares the uterine environment for **implantation** of a fertilized egg. This stage lasts about eight to ten days. If a fertilized egg is not received, estrogen and progesterone levels decrease, signaling the breakdown of the uterine lining, which is shed during the final phase of the cycle, **menstruation**.

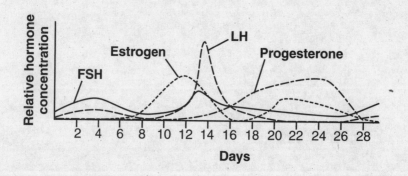

LESSON 9
HEREDITY

THE LAWS OF HEREDITY

Genetics is the study of heredity, a study of how certain characteristics are passed on from parents to children. The basic principles of heredity were first discovered in the nineteenth century by **Gregor Mendel**. Since then, the field of genetics has expanded greatly. In order to understand Mendel's work, you will first need to brush up on some genetics vocabulary.

Genes: Each trait—an expressed characteristic—is produced by a pair of hereditary factors collectively known as **genes**. Within a chromosome, there are many genes, each of which controls the inheritance of a particular trait. A gene is a segment of a chromosome that produces a particular trait. For example, in pea plants, there's a gene on the chromosome that holds the code for seed coat. The position of a gene on a chromosome is called its **locus.**

Alleles: A gene usually consists of a *pair* of hereditary factors called **alleles**. Each organism carries two alleles for a particular trait. Another way to say this is that two alleles make up a gene, which in turn produces a particular trait.

Dominant and Recessive Alleles: An allele can be **dominant** or **recessive**. In simple cases, an organism expresses either the dominant or recessive trait. For example, a plant can be tall or short. The convention is to assign a capital and a lowercase of the same letter for the two alleles: The dominant allele receives the capital letter, and the recessive allele receives the lowercase letter. For example, if tallness is dominant in your family, you might give the dominant allele a T for tall, and a t for the short recessive allele.

Phenotype and Genotype: When discussing the physical appearance of an organism, one refers to its **phenotype.** The phenotype tells one what the organism looks like. When talking about the genetic makeup of an organism, one refers to its **genotype.** The genotype tells one which alleles the organism possesses.

Homozygous and Heterozygous: When an organism has two identical alleles for a given trait, one says that the organism is **homozygous.** For instance, TT and tt would both represent the genotypes of homozygous organisms, one homozygous dominant and the other homozygous recessive. If an organism has two *different* alleles for a given trait, say Tt, that organism is **heterozygous.**

Parent and Filial Generations: The first generation is always called the **parent** or **P1** generation. The offspring of the **P1** generation are called the **filial** or **F1** generation, and the offspring of the F1 generation are the **F2** generation.

Mendelian Genetics

Okay, now it's time to put that vocabulary to the test. For example, because you receive an earlobe gene from each parent, you have two genes that influence your phenotype (physical appearance) for earlobes. In this case, the phenotype for unattached earlobes (U) is dominant over the phenotype for attached earlobes (u).

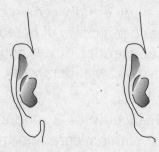

Unattached   Attached

The genotypes (genetic makeup) UU and Uu both result in unattached earlobes. Parents whose genotypes are either UU or uu are homozygous for the earlobe attachment trait. This type of cross is called a **monohybrid cross**—it constitutes a study of only one trait. In this case, the trait is earlobe shape.

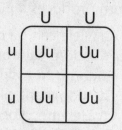

Individuals whose genotype is Uu are heterozygous for the earlobe attachment trait. However, because U is dominant over u, all heterozygous individuals will have unattached earlobes. So, what's the statistical *probability* of having a child with attached earlobes? In this case (one parent UU, the other uu), there is no chance of having a child with attached earlobes even though a homozygous recessive parent (uu) is available going into the cross. To better understand this genotype/phenotype business, you can rely on the help of a **Punnett square**. The Punnett square is nothing more than a multiplication table using letters to represent genotypes.

Now try another one:

If one of the heterozygous children from this F1 generation has a homozygous recessive spouse, what's the *probability* that one of their children (F2) will have attached earlobes?

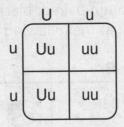

The second couple has a 50 percent chance of having a child with attached earlobes, because each parent, one homozygous recessive and the other heterozygous, has the potential to contribute the recessive genes necessary for that phenotype to appear in their children.

From these two examples you may have surmised the following:

$$\text{Probability} = \frac{\text{number of possible outcomes}}{\text{total number of all possible outcomes}}$$

Okay, what is the *probability* of having children with attached earlobes when both parents are heterozygous for earlobe attachment?

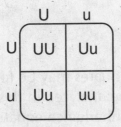

THE LAW OF INDEPENDENT ASSORTMENT

As a result of countless experiments on pea plants, Mendel came up with the **law of independent assortment,** which states that each gene is inherited separately from others. But what happens when you have two different traits at the same time? How do you represent that in a Punnett square? Well, you just have to make the table a bit bigger.

Take a look at an example—in this case guinea pigs.

Some guinea pigs have rough hair and some have smooth hair. It turns out that rough hair (R) is the dominant gene, and smooth hair (r) is the recessive one. Some guinea pigs also have black ear tips (B), which is the dominant trait, and some of them have white ear tips (b), which is recessive. These genes are going to be inherited totally independently of each other.

What happens if a heterozygous rough-haired, black-eared guinea pig is mated with another one just like it. Take a look at the following diagram to see what happens:

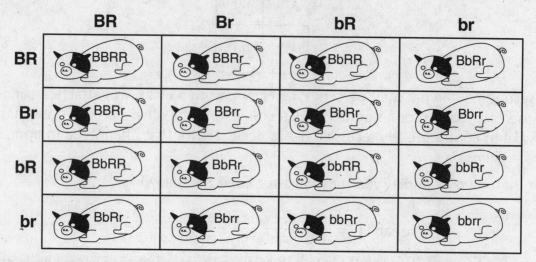

This is a **dihybrid cross.** If you wanted to look at three traits at the same time, it would take 64 squares! Just imagine how many squares it would take to do a Punnett square for all your traits.

BEYOND MENDELIAN GENETICS

As fun, fast, and clear as Punnett squares may be for predicting patterns of inheritance, only a few traits can be analyzed in this way. All sorts of things can throw a monkey wrench into the inheritance equation, resulting in more complex patterns of heredity.

Here are a couple of examples of non-Mendelian forms of inheritance.

- **Incomplete dominance:** In some cases, the traits will blend. For example, if you cross a white snapdragon plant (dominant) and a red snapdragon plant (recessive), the result will be a pink snapdragon plant.
- **Codominance:** Sometimes, you'll see an equal expression of both alleles. For example, an individual can have an AB blood type. In this case, each allele is equally expressed. That is, both the A allele and the B allele are expressed. That's why the person is said to have an AB blood type.

The only remaining factor to affect inheritance patterns is **mutation.**

LESSON 10
DNA

BACK TO BASICS: DNA STRUCTURE

Now that you know how reproduction occurs, you can divert your attention to the material that genes are made of. DNA can be thought of as the hereditary blueprint of the cell. The DNA of a cell is contained in structures called chromosomes, which you've already read about. Within each chromosome are genes, which control hereditary factors. The chromosomes are basically enormous coils of DNA and associated proteins called **histones**. Found inside the nucleus, chromosomes direct and control all the activities necessary for life.

THE STRUCTURE OF DNA

The DNA molecule consists of two long, connected strands in the shape of a twisted ladder called a double helix.

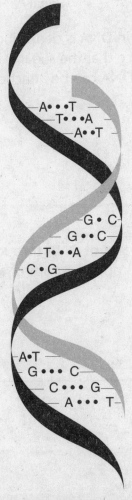

Revealing the structure of DNA was no picnic. The first person to carry out studies on the nuclei of cells was **Frederick Meischer** in 1868. Meischer analyzed the nuclei of white blood cells in pus on discarded surgical bandages. (Gross!) He detected a phosphorus-containing substance that he called nuclein. For the next eighty years, scientists were developing their understanding of the composition and structure of DNA. Finally, in 1953, **James Watson** and **Francis Crick** first determined the double helix structure of DNA.

Each strand of DNA is made up of repeating subunits called nucleotides. Each nucleotide consists of a sugar, a phosphate, and a nitrogenous base. The following is a simplified schematic of a nucleotide:

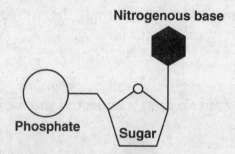

The name of the five-carbon sugar in DNA is deoxyribose, which is where the name *deoxyribo*nucleic comes from. Notice that the sugar is linked to two things: a phosphate group and a base. A nucleotide in DNA can be attached to one of the following four bases:

- adenine
- guanine
- cytosine
- thymine

A single strand

The nucleotides link in a single strand of DNA through their phosphate groups. Here's a very simple diagram of a small section of a DNA strand.

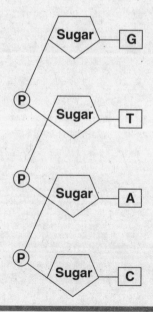

So, how do these subunits differ? What separates one nucleotide from the next if all nucleotides are made of a sugar, a phosphate, and a nitrogenous base? The key to the puzzle is the nitrogenous base. Regardless of the shape, size, kingdom, or function, the DNA of all life on Earth is made from the same four nitrogenous bases. It is the differences in the sequences of these bases that result in genetic differences and differences in proteins.

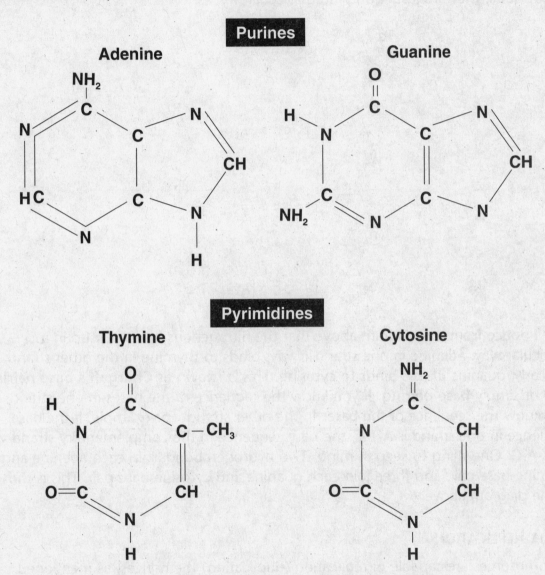

The double strand

Now, take a look at the way in which two DNA strands are joined to form the double helix. Remember, you can think of DNA as a ladder. The sides of the ladder consist of alternating sugar and phosphate groups, while the rungs of the ladder consist of pairs of nitrogenous bases joined by hydrogen bonds. Hydrogen bonds are not really bonds at all; they are just strong intermolecular forces.

You'll notice from the diagram above that the nitrogenous bases pair up in a particular way. Adenine in one strand *always* binds to thymine in the other strand. Similarly, guanine *always* binds to cytosine. This is known as **Chargaff's base pairing rule** or simply **base pairing.** If you know the sequence of the bases in one strand, you know the sequence of the bases in the other strand. For example, if the base sequence in one strand is A-T-C, the base sequence in the complementary strand will be T-A-G. One thing to keep in mind: Two hydrogen bonds join each adenine and thymine base pair, and three join each guanine and cytosine base pair. This is shown in the diagram above.

DNA REPLICATION

Chromosomes are capable of replicating (duplicating) themselves, as mentioned earlier. In fact, you may even remember that they do this during interphase. Because the DNA molecule is twisted in a double helix configuration, the first step in DNA replication is the unwinding of the double helix and the breaking of the hydrogen bonds between the strands. This is accomplished through the use of enzymes. Next, using the now single strands of DNA as a **template,** or blueprint, DNA **polymerases** move along both single-stranded DNA molecules, adding complementary bases to the exposed nucleotides on each strand. After the new complementary strands are complete, they twist with their respective template strands, forming two complete DNA molecules.

You would think that the trickiest thing a cell would have to do would be to duplicate the DNA inside the cell. After all, errors during DNA replication and cellular reproduction could potentially result in **mutation**. You will read more about mutation later on in this lesson.

PROTEINS AND THE GENETIC CODE

DNA is crucial to the day-to-day operations of the cell. Without it, the cell would not be able to direct the production of proteins that regulate all the activities of the cell. However, DNA does not directly manufacture proteins. This job falls to an intermediate known as **ribonucleic acid (RNA)**.

RNA carries out the instructions of DNA, so the order of events looks like the following:

$$\text{DNA} \xrightarrow{\text{(Transcription)}} \text{RNA} \xrightarrow{\text{(Translation)}} \text{Proteins}$$

The above is referred to as the central dogma of molecular biology. Information is passed from DNA to RNA, which then handles the production of polypeptides (don't forget that polypeptide is simply a fancy name for proteins. You'll see why in just a bit). But before you read about the way in which RNA makes proteins, you'll need to learn a little about its structure. RNA differs from DNA in the following three principal ways:

1. RNA is single stranded, not double stranded.
2. The five-carbon sugar in RNA is **ribose**, not deoxyribose.
3. The nitrogenous bases in RNA are adenine, guanine, cytosine, and **uracil**. Uracil replaces thymine in RNA.

Here's a table to help you memorize the differences between DNA and RNA.

Differences between DNA and RNA		
	DNA (double stranded)	**RNA (single stranded)**
Sugar	deoxyribose	ribose
Bases	adenine guanine cytosine thymine	adenine guanine cytosine uracil

Types of RNA

There are three types of RNA: **messenger RNA (mRNA)**, **ribosomal RNA (rRNA)**, and **transfer RNA (tRNA).** All three types of RNA are key players in the synthesis of proteins. Messenger RNA carries the information from DNA after the process of transcription, which you'll read about in a minute. Ribosomal RNA makes up the ribosomes, the primary sites of protein synthesis in the cytoplasm. Transfer RNA shuttles amino acids around the cell, bringing them into place at the ribosome. With this information, you can move on to transcription.

Transcription: Synthesis of mRNA

As you just read, DNA transcribes its information into RNA, which travels out of the nucleus (into the cytoplasm) to undergo translation to a polypeptide. As is the case with DNA replication, the strand of DNA must first split, and transcription begins—the nucleotides that make up the new RNA molecule take their places one at a time along the template, forming temporary hydrogen bonds with DNA. But in mRNA synthesis, only one strand of DNA acts as a template. When transcription is complete, the new mRNA strand peels away from the DNA template, which allows the DNA to rezip as its hydrogen bonds are formed again. Don't forget—uracil takes the place of thymine in RNA.

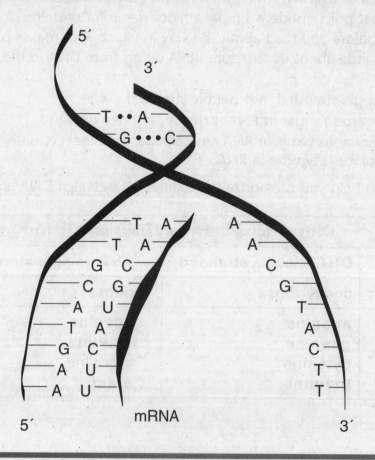

TRANSLATION: PROTEIN SYNTHESIS

At this point, mRNA travels out of the nucleus into the cytoplasm. The mRNA molecule carries the message from DNA in the form of **codons,** which are groups of three bases, each of which corresponds to one of twenty amino acids. Codons are very specific. For example, the sequence A-U-G found on an mRNA molecule corresponds to the amino acid methionine.

The mRNA finds a ribosome in the cytoplasm and attaches itself to wait for the appropriate amino acid to pass by. This is where tRNA comes in. One end of the tRNA binds to an amino acid. The other end, called an **anticodon,** has three nitrogenous bases that pair up with the bases contained in the codon.

Transfer RNA is the go-between in protein synthesis. Each tRNA molecule picks up an amino acid in the cell's cytoplasm and shuttles it to the ribosome. For example, the tRNA with the anticodon U-A-C is methionine's personal shuttle. It carries no other amino acid. This way, every time mRNA shows a codon of A-U-G, it is certain to pick up only methionine.

BUT WHERE'S THE PROTEIN?

Remember that the mRNA contains many thousands of codons, or triplets, of nucleotide bases. As each amino acid is brought to the mRNA, it is linked up by the formation of a peptide bond. And when many amino acids link up, a **polypeptide** is formed.

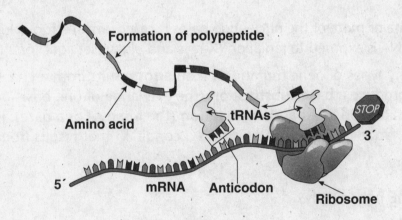

THE ONE GENE–ONE POLYPEPTIDE HYPOTHESIS

A gene is a region of the chromosome that codes for a particular trait. Now that you've read about protein synthesis and the role of proteins in the cell, you can think of the definition of a gene in a slightly more specific way. Because proteins direct the processes of the cell, a gene is therefore a region of DNA that codes for a single polypeptide.

This is known as the **one gene–one polypeptide** hypothesis, and it comes a little nearer to the true definition of a gene. Remember, to define genes simply in terms of traits leads to some confusion. Some traits are the consequence of the interaction of several genes. However, when a gene is defined as a region of the genetic code that codes for a specific polypeptide, it's much easier to pinpoint where one gene begins and where the other ends.

MUTATIONS

A cell uses some twenty amino acids to construct its proteins. However, errors occasionally occur during DNA replication that cause the amino acids to be attached in the incorrect order. For example, suppose a short segment of a template DNA strand has the sequence T-A-C. The complementary DNA segment should be A-T-G. If for some reason another thymine is inserted in the last position instead of guanine, the new strand of DNA would read A-T-T, and this would lead to the insertion of the wrong amino acid in the protein. One error of this sort is enough to inactivate the entire protein!

A change in one or more of the nucleotide bases is called a **mutation.** Mutations can occur when DNA is exposed to radiation (X-rays and ultraviolet light) or chemical agents.

There are many types of gene mutations. If an error results from a change in a single base, it may produce a **base substitution** (the exchange of one base for another), an **addition** (the addition of a base), or **deletion** (the removal of a base). For example, albinism—the lack of skin pigmentation—is a condition that results from a change in a single gene.

CHROMOSOME MUTATIONS

Mutations can also occur on a grander scale in chromosomes. Sometimes, a set of chromosomes has an extra or missing member. This can occur because of **nondisjunction,** the failure of the chromosomes to separate properly during the crossover in meiosis. Errors like these produce the wrong number of chromosomes in a cell, which results in severe genetic defects. For example, Down's syndrome, a form of mental disability with characteristic physical impairments, results from the presence of an extra twenty-first chromosome. An individual afflicted with Down's syndrome has three rather than two copies of this single chromosome.

Chromosomal abnormalities also occur when a segment of a chromosome breaks. The most common examples are **translocation** (when a segment of a chromosome moves to another chromosome), **inversion** (when a segment of a chromosome is inserted in the reverse orientation), and **deletion** (when a segment of a chromosome is lost).

MANIPULATING THE CODE

Modern technology allows scientists to manipulate genetic information either indirectly by **artificial selection** or directly by **genetic engineering.**

There are a number of techniques that can indirectly manipulate the inheritance of genes in plants and animals. In artificial selection, desirable characteristics are bred into populations. This is accomplished by allowing only those organisms with the desired characteristics to interbreed. For example, by hand-pollinating flowers, rose breeders have produced thousands of new roses. Other breeding techniques include **hybridization** (in which animals are crossbred to maximize the favorable traits of both varieties of a given species) and **inbreeding** (to produce pure breeds). Examples of these breeding patterns are found in corn, flowers, fruit, cattle, and dogs, among others.

Scientists have found new ways of altering organisms through the **transfer** of individual genes from one organism to another in a process known as genetic engineering. In genetic engineering, DNA is cut out of one gene and transferred to another. The host DNA is now called **recombinant DNA.** When the cell undergoes protein synthesis, it will read the inserted portion of DNA as if it were its own, and this leads to the production of specific proteins.

This technique has resulted in the successful production of large amounts of proteins such as insulin and growth hormone. For example, the DNA that instructs a human cell to make insulin can be transferred to a bacterium. As this bacterium divides, it passes the gene for insulin to its offspring. Pretty soon you've got millions upon millions of bacteria churning out insulin. Once it's isolated from the solution in which the bacteria are raised, the insulin can be used by diabetics to help regulate their blood sugar.

LOOKING FOR DEFECTS

Many genetic defects are detectable even before an organism is born. Researchers and doctors use several techniques to identify such defects. You should be familiar with the following terms just in case one of them pops up in a question on the exam:

- **Genetic screening:** a technique used to identify abnormal conditions by detecting the presence or absence of certain chemicals in the blood or urine.

- **Amniocentesis:** a technique in which a sample of amniotic fluid is taken from the mother's womb. In the amniotic fluid is an abundance of fetal cells. By examining the fetal cells, doctors can detect severe disorders that might pose a risk to the fetus.

- **Karyotyping:** a technique in which paired chromosomes are arranged based on their shape and size. The chromosomes below are organized into a human karyotype.

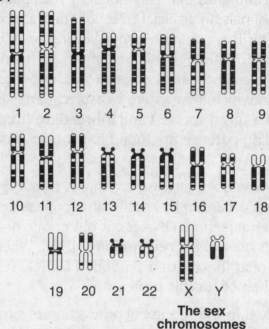

The sex chromosomes

This procedure helps to identify such chromosomal abnormalities as extra or missing chromosomes.

GENETIC DISORDERS

Here's a list of some genetic disorders you should also be aware of.

- **Phenylketonuria (PKU):** A genetic disorder in which the body is unable to metabolize the amino acid phenylalanine. This condition may lead to mental disability.

- **Sickle-cell anemia:** A genetic disorder in which red blood cells are abnormally shaped and have trouble traveling through the capillary beds.

- **Tay-Sachs disease:** A genetic disorder in which the nervous system malfunctions due to the accumulation of fat in the brain.

DNA TECHNOLOGIES

Some of the most exciting work in science today is happening in the world of molecular biology. Through genetic engineering, scientists have been able to influence fields ranging from medicine to agriculture.

A return to *Jurassic Park*

As fantastic as the premise of the movie *Jurassic Park* sounded, it's really not all that far-fetched. The transfer of isolated genes from one organism to another in order to increase protein production or to alter the protein products of the organism is the heart and soul of **genetic engineering.** Genetic engineering involves building **recombinant DNA,** or DNA constructed from the DNA of different organisms. Sounds like Dr. Frankenstein started working on a molecular level, eh? And now you're left wondering, "How'd they do that?" Well, most scientists have turned to a trusted and valued friend—bacteria—to help create recombinant DNA. With their simple circular DNA molecule, they help to make some pretty interesting things happen.

BIOTECHNOLOGY 101

Step 1: Cut a gene from the DNA source using restriction enzymes or polymerase chain reaction (PCR) technology. Restriction enzymes are special enzymes that identify specific base sequences in DNA and then chop up the DNA according to the specific sequence. For example, *Eco* R1 is a restriction enzyme that recognizes the base sequence GAATTC and cleaves DNA with this sequence into fragments with short, sticky ends that can be attached to other fragments. PCR uses specialized enzymes and additional nucleotides to make copies of specific gene regions. In either case, a gene then becomes available for Step 2.

Step 2: The gene made available through the processes described in Step 1 is then inserted into a vector, a molecular middleman of sorts, that carries the gene into bacterial cells where it fuses with the bacterial DNA.

Step 3: Bacteria now do what they do best—reproduce. With the implanted gene inside, they grow and produce perhaps millions of clones, or genetically identical copies of your gene.

Step 4: Bacterial cells that contain the gene insert are then identified through restriction digests with the help of gel electrophoresis, a technique used to visualize DNA fragments produced using restriction enzymes.

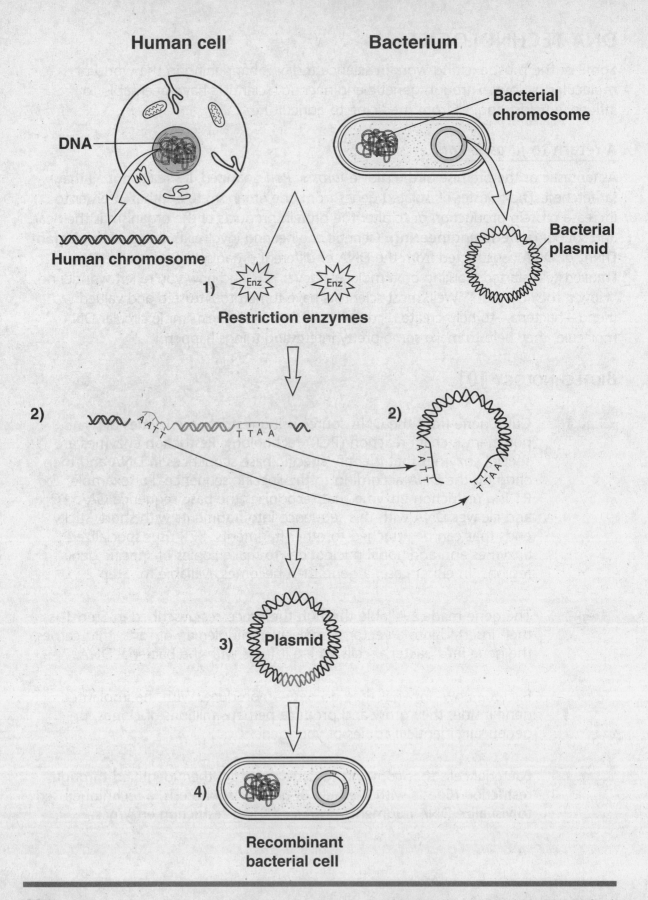

Human cell

Bacterium

Bacterial chromosome

DNA

Human chromosome

Bacterial plasmid

1) Enz   Enz

Restriction enzymes

2)   A A T T   T T A A

2)   A A T T   T T A A

3)   **Plasmid**

4)   **Recombinant bacterial cell**

OTHER APPLICATIONS FOR PCR AND RFLP

The **Human Genome Project** is perhaps one of the most ambitious undertakings that employs biotechnology and gene-sequencing. The goal of the Human Genome Project is to identify and locate the entire collection of genes in a human cell.

Although science knows that it is the differences in DNA sequence or order that separates one organism from the next, not every gene in every organism is different from every other. **Conserved** genes are those genes whose base sequence is the same across many types of **phyla.** The results of this technique, particularly when coupled with analyses of restriction enzyme maps of DNA, also known as **restriction fragment polymorphism (RFLP),** has rapidly become the molecular analysis tool of choice for forensic scientists, evolutionary biologists, and molecular conservationists. On a gel, fragments are separated according to their size (molecular weight), creating sets of fragments that may be used to identify genetic similarities and differences between organisms.

So, where does all this very nifty molecular technology take you? Just about any place you want to go.

As you can see, molecular techniques and genetic recombinants are handy little study tools in the lab, but they are also affecting everyday life as well.

Medicine

Not since the discovery of vaccines has a medical discovery made so much of an impact as that of recombinant technology. As a matter of fact, recombinant technology has been used to generate new medicines, provide vaccines against disease, and establish the foundation for **gene therapy.** Gene therapy is used to treat persons afflicted with genetic disorders, such as cystic fibrosis and immune disorders, by inserting copies of normal genes to replace defective genes.

Agriculture

Although there is a lot of attention on the use of biotechnology for human health issues, plants and other animals have not escaped the eye of the genetic engineering community. Genetic engineering is currently improving crop resistance to insects and disease, thereby improving crop yields while reducing the need for insecticides and herbicides.

The meat industry also has a stake in genetic engineering. Genetically engineered growth hormones added to the diets of hogs, beef, and dairy cows have increased the amount of meat and milk produced. However, many have debated whether genetically engineered foods are safe for regular human consumption.

Comparing DNA sequences

Today, scientists have the molecular tools necessary to determine relationships between organisms and between species. The study of these relationships is called **systematics.** DNA sequencing is the most precise and powerful method available for comparing DNA. Once the actual nucleotide sequences of comparable gene regions have been determined for two organisms or species, it is possible to use these data to infer evolutionary relationships, including relationships between species and relationships within populations of species.

Because the linear arrangement of amino acids in a polypeptide is determined by the base sequence of a gene, a close match in the amino acid sequence of two proteins from different species indicates that the two species are closely related. Basically, the greater the difference between amino acid sequences, the greater the evolutionary distance between the two species.

REVIEW FOR LESSONS 8–10

Take a few moments to practice test-taking strategies for questions about reproduction and genetics. The answers and explanations are on page 129.

1 In canaries, the gene for singing (S) is dominant over the gene for nonsinging (s). When a heterozygous singing canary is mated with a nonsinging canary, what percentage of the offspring is likely to possess the singing trait?

   A 0%

   B 25%

   C 50%

   D 100%

2 Heterozygous pink snapdragons are an example of incomplete dominance in plants. These pink-flowered plants may be produced as a result of—

   F a cross between parent plants whose flower colors are different from that of their offspring

   G the expression of a dominant gene

   H the expression of a recessive gene

   J a cross between parent plants, both of which have flowers with white petals

3 The production of motile haploid gametes takes place in the—

   A ureters

   B ovaries

   C male gonads

   D gastric glands

4 The chart below shows the genotype of four babies with regard to blood type.

Baby	Genotype
W	$I^A I^A$
X	$I^B I^B$
Y	ii
Z	$I^A I^B$

Which baby could *not* be the child of parents who both have AB blood?

   F W

   G X

   H Y

   J Z

5 Which of the following molecules is found in RNA molecules but not in DNA molecules—

A phosphate

B adenine

C uracil

D thymine

6 In which situation could a mutation be passed on to the offspring of an organism?

F Ultraviolet light causes uncontrolled cell growth in skin cells.

G The DNA of a human lung cell undergoes random breakage.

H A human sex cell forms a gamete containing twenty-four chromosomes.

J The chromosomes in a cell of the uterine wall change.

ANSWERS AND EXPLANATIONS

1 **C 50%.** If you draw a Punnett square, you can see that 50 percent of the offspring would possess the singing trait.

2 **F a cross between parent plants whose flower colors are different from that of their offspring. G** and **H** are false, because neither allele is dominant or recessive in incomplete dominance. Expression of each allele is modified by the expression of the other. Crossing white flowers would only produce white flowers, so **J** is incorrect.

3 **C male gonads.** Self-propelled gametes are sperm cells and are produced in male reproductive structures (aka gonads). Ovaries, **B,** produce female gametes. **A** and **D** are not involved in reproduction.

4 **H Y.** Any time you appear to be faced with a question governed by Mendelian genetics, draw a figure. If you know that *ii* represents the double recessive type O condition, then you may not need to draw anything. In any case, AB parents cannot have type O children. **F, G,** and **J** are possible.

5 **C uracil.** Both RNA and DNA molecules are attached to a phosphate group, so **A** is wrong. As for **B** and **D,** thymine and adenine are bases found in RNA as well as DNA.

6 **H A human sex cell forms a gamete containing twenty-four chromosomes.** The question is really just asking when a mutation can be inherited. The answer is when it takes place in either the egg or the sperm. **F, G,** and **J** are mutations in somatic (body) cells. Only gametes (sex cells) can carry hereditary information.

LESSON 11
TAXONOMY

TAXONOMY

Taxonomy is a branch of biology that deals with the naming and classifying of life-forms. Taxonomists classify organisms based on similar structural and molecular characteristics. There are at least seven levels of classification for each identified organism.

Kingdom, Phylum, Class, Order, Family, Genus, Species

Less in common →→→→→→→→→→→ **More in common**

You can see that as you go from level to level, the similarities between the organisms increase. So, if two different organisms are classified within the same species, it would mean that both organisms are considered close relatives.

The following is a mnemonic to help you get through the jargon:

King Philip Came Over For Good Soup

Remember:
- Each kingdom is made up of many phyla.
- Each phylum is made up of many classes.
- Each class is made up of many orders.
- Each order is made up of many families.
- Each family is made up of many genuses.
- Each genus is made up of many species.

Taxonomists also use a branching diagram to illustrate the phylagenetic relationships between groups of organisms.

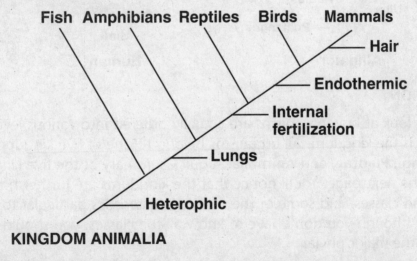

When two branches of the diagram meet at a certain point, this represents the shared characteristics between the two groups.

In order to accurately classify organisms, biologists must be able to distinguish between **homologous** and **analogous structures**. Although birds and insects both have wings, these groups do not have a common ancestor. The evolution of wings was a separate event in each group. So, even though the wings perform the same function for each organism, they are considered to be *analogous* structures.

Bird wing   **Insect wing**

On the other hand, the wings of birds and bats, the arms of humans, and the flippers of whales are all *homologous* structures, suggesting a common ancestor. A common ancestor is inferred because of the similar construction of these limbs from the same skeletal elements: humerus, radius, ulna, and phalanges (digits).

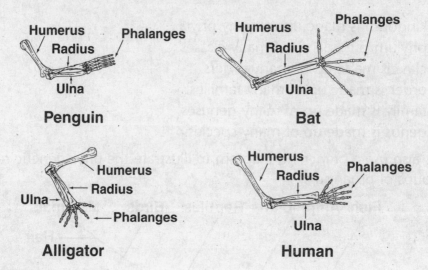

CLASSIFICATION

Take a closer look at how organisms are actually ordered into various levels. The highest level is the kingdom. All organisms belong to one of five kingdoms: **Monera, Protista, Fungi, Plantae,** and **Animalia**. A quick summary of the five kingdoms appears on the next page. You'll notice that the kingdoms are further broken down into phyla and classes, and some of the main characteristics particular to each are mentioned. Although you don't have to know all the classes, you should be familiar with at least the major phyla.

The 5 Kingdoms	Characteristics	Ecological Role
1. Monera	Prokaryotes (lack distinct nuclei and other membranous organelles); single-celled; microscopic	
Bacteria	Cell walls composed of peptidoglycan (a substance derived from amino acids and sugars); cells may be spherical (cocci), rod-shaped (bacilli), or coiled (spirilla)	Decomposers; some chemosynthetic autotrophs; important in recycling nitrogen and other elements; a few are photosynthetic, usually employing hydrogen sulfide as hydrogen source; some are pathogenic (cause disease)
Cyanobacteria	Photosynthetic; previously known as blue-green algae	Producers; blooms (population explosion) associated with water polution
2. Protista	Eukaryotes; mainly unicellular or colonial	
Protozoa	Microscopic; unicellular; depend upon diffusion to support many of their metabolic activities	Important part of zooplankton; near base of many food chains
Eukaryotic algae	Some are difficult to differentiate from the protozoa; some have brown pigment in addition to chlorophyll	Very important producers, especially in marine and freshwater ecosystems
Slime molds	Protozoan characteristics during part of life cycle; fungal traits during remainder	
3. Fungi	Eukaryotes; plantlike but lack chlorophyll and cannot carry on photosynthesis	Decomposers, probably to an even greater extent than bacteria; some are pathogenic (e.g., athlete's foot is caused by a fungus)
Molds, yeasts, mildew, mushrooms	Body composed of threadlike hyphae; rarely discrete cells	Some used in food (yeasts used in making bread and alcoholic beverages); responsible for much spoilage and crop loss
4. Plantae	Multicellular eukaryotes; adapted for photosynthesis; photosynthetic cells have chloroplasts; all plants have reproductive tissues or organs and pass through distinct developmental stages and alterations of generations; cell walls of cellulose; cells often have large central vacuole	Other organisms depend upon plants to produce foodstuff and molecular oxygen
5. Animalia	Multicellular eukaryotic heterotrophs many of which exhibit advanced tissue differentiation and complex organ systems; lack cell walls; extremely and quickly responsive to stimuli, with specialized nervous tissue to coordinate responses; determinate growth	Almost the sole consuming organisms in the biosphere, some being specialized herbivores, carnivores, and detrivores (eating dead organisms or organic material such as dead leaves)

CLASSIFICATION OF FUNGI

Phylum	Characteristics	Examples	
Fungi	Lack chlorophyll; produce spores	Molds, yeasts, mildew, mushrooms	

CLASSIFICATION OF ANIMALS

Phylum	Characteristics	Examples	
1. Porifera	Two layers of cells with pores	Sponge	
2. Coelenterata	Two layers of cells; hollow digestive cavity with tentacles	Hydra, jellyfish	
3. Platyhelminthes (Flatworms)	Three layers of cells; flat; bilateral symmetry	Tapeworm, planaria, fluke	
4. Nematoda (Roundworms)	Digestive system with a mouth and anus; round	Hookworm	
5. Rotifera	Digestive system	Rotifer	
6. Annelida (Segmented worms)	Long, segmented body; digestive system; closed circulatory system	Earthworm	
7. Mollusca	Soft body; hard shell	Clam, snail	
8. Arthropoda **Class**	Segmented body; jointed legs; exoskeleton		
Crustacea	Gills for breathing; jointed legs	Crab, lobster	
Insecta	Three body parts; one pair of antennae; six legs; tracheal breathing system	Bee, grasshopper	
Arachnida	Two body parts; eight legs	Spider	
Chilopoda	One pair of legs per segment	Centipede	
Diplopoda	Two pairs of legs per segment	Millipede	
9. Echinodermata (Spiny-skinned)	Spiny exoskeleton; complete digestive system	Starfish, sea urchin, sea cucumber	

CLASSIFICATION OF ANIMALS (Continued)

Phylum	Characteristics	Examples	
10. Chordata	Notochord; dorsal nerve cord; gill slits		
Subphylum Vertebrate	Backbone		
Class Pisces (fish)	Gills; scales; two-chambered heart	Salmon	
Amphibia	Breathe through gills, lungs, and thin, moist skin; three-chambered heart	Frog	
Reptilia	Eggs with a chitinous covering; cold-blooded; scales; three-chambered heart	Snake	
Aves	Warm-blooded; four-chambered heart; eggs with shell; wings	Owl	
Mammalia	Warm-blooded; hair; produce milk to feed young	Human, kangaroo	

CLASSIFICATION OF PLANTS

Phylum	Characteristics	Examples	
1. Bryophyta	No true roots and stems; produce spores	Liverworts	
		Mosses	
2. Tracheophyta	True roots, stems, and leaves; contain a vascular system	Flowering plants	

MODERN CLASSIFICATIONS

Closely related organisms pass through similar stages during their embryologic development. For example, both fish and humans are **vertebrates**—animals characterized by a backbone. Beyond this shared characteristic, fish would seem to have very little in common with humans, but the embryologic development tells a different story. The embryologic developments of all vertebrates, from fish to humans, are characterized by gill pouches, a tail, and limb buds. As indicated in the diagram below, these common structures develop into distinctive features for each organism. However, it is the similarities between these embryonic structures that unify different classes of fish, amphibians, reptiles, birds, and mammals into the same phylum: **chordata.**

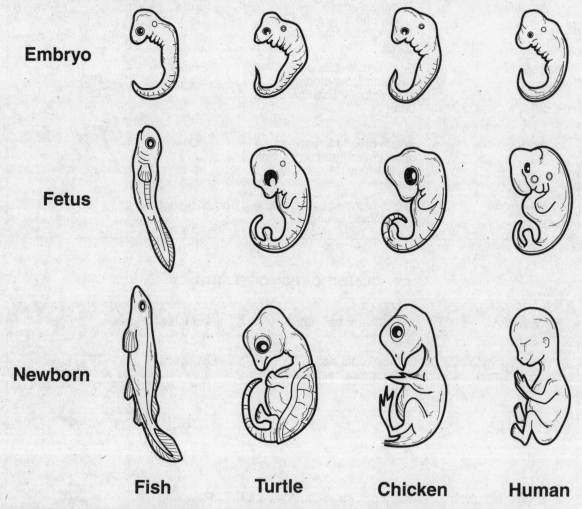

Embryo			
Fetus			
Newborn			
Fish	Turtle	Chicken	Human

Taxonomy used to be the primary domain of zoologists and embryologists. However, like so many other fields in science, the field of taxonomy is also reaping the benefits of advances in molecular biology and biotechnology. Protein and DNA sequence analyses have contributed significantly to the classification of organisms. In some cases, molecular evidence has caused biologists to completely reclassify modern and extinct species.

LESSON 12
INTERACTION OF LIFE-FORMS

THE AGENTS OF DISEASE

The primary goal of all living things is to find and secure suitable resources such as food, shelter, and mates. These goals all serve the purpose of increasing the probability that their genes will be passed on to the next generation. Some species have developed strategies whereby their greatest success for securing resources comes through reliance on other organisms. Unfortunately, the reliance of certain microorganisms on plant and animal hosts, including humans, often causes disease.

BACTERIA

Although bacteria is helpful to humans in many ways, when it comes to human diseases, no single group of organisms has created more human misery than bacteria. Bacteria have been the primary offenders of such historical outbreaks as the bubonic plague of the Middle Ages, cholera, and typhoid fever. Many common or formerly common human diseases are the result of infections by parasitic bacteria that attack cells and secrete toxins. **Alexander Fleming**'s discovery of penicillin in 1928 led to the development of antibiotics in the 1940s and the effective treatment of such bacterial infections as tuberculosis, pneumonia, and middle ear infections. However, the overuse of antibiotics has caused health professionals to begin reevaluating the blanket use of antibiotics, because many bacteria have developed drug-resistant strains. It is becoming increasingly difficult to treat bacterial infections as drug-resistant strains of bacteria defy treatment with standard antibiotics.

VIRUSES

Viruses are on the flip side of the microorganism coin. Like infectious bacteria, viral infections have been a bane to human existence for millenia. They have caused such historical epidemics as smallpox, polio, influenza, and are the causative agents in acquired immune deficiency syndrome (AIDS). Unlike bacteria that respond to antibiotics, viruses defy standard medical treatments.

PROTISTS

Although not all protists are **parasites** (organisms that inhabit other organisms and are harmful to the host in which they live), some protists can cause serious diseases in plants and animals. The Great Irish Potato Famine (1845–1847), which caused the deaths of more than 400,000 people, was caused by a protist that infected potato plants. Other diseases linked to protists, such as toxoplasmosis, have severe health implications for unborn children. Some parasitic protists, *Entamoeba* for example, infect humans directly through contaminated food and water supplies and cause amoebic dysentery. Others utilize humans and other animals as secondary hosts for the completion of their life cycles. The parasitic protist *Plasmodium* infects mosquitoes of the genus *Anopheles*, which then become the agents of infectious disease, spreading the malaria-causing protist from one human host to the next.

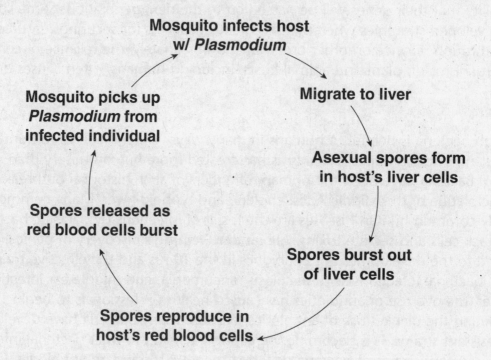

FUNGI

Although most fungi are free-living heterotrophs that contribute significantly to nutrient cycling as decomposers, there are also certain fungi able to cause disease in humans. Common human fungal infections include thrush, athlete's foot, and ringworm. Fungal infections like those caused by powdery mildews, rusts, and smut cost farmers millions of dollars each year in decreased crop yields and fungicide sprays.

The worms move in, the worms move out . . .

Not all parasites are microorganisms. Flatworms represent the largest group of parasitic macroorganisms, with more than 6,000 species in all. Similar to parasitic protists, flukes and tapeworms also utilize a human host intermediate.

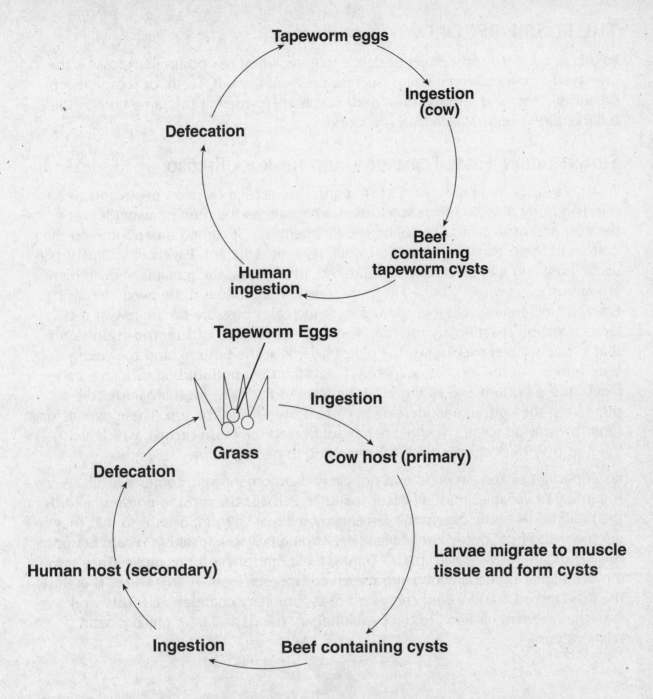

Other plant and animal parasites include over fifty species of roundworms. Infection by *Trichinella* causes trichinosis in humans who consume undercooked or poorly cooked pork. Other common parasitic roundworms include the intestinal roundworm *Ascaris* and hookworms, such as *Necator*.

THE FOSSIL RECORD

Fossils provide the most direct evidence that evolution has occurred. A fossil is the preserved or mineralized remains, such as the bones, shells, teeth, or footprints of organisms that lived in the distant past. Fossils are formed at the same time as the sedimentary rocks in which they are found.

SEDIMENTATION, FOSSIL FORMATION, AND THE ROCK RECORD

Weathered rock fragments, called **sediments**, are carried by rivers or streams to a standing body of water, such as a lake or an ocean. As the running water leaves the river and moves into the ocean, the sediment that it carried is deposited on the bottom of the ocean, forming a horizontal layer of sediment. Layers of sediment pile up as more and more sediment is deposited. In addition, the remains of dead marine organisms are eventually buried as more sediment continues to be piled on. Over time, the increasing weight of the top layer increases pressure on the lowest rock layers, creating sedimentary rock and fossils. The **principle of superposition** states that in undisturbed rock layers, the oldest layer is at the bottom, and the youngest layer is found at the top. Subsequently, fossils found in undisturbed rock layers are oldest at the bottom and youngest at the top. Additionally, fossil organisms are simplest at the bottom and increase in complexity toward the top. These two factors together provide scientists with a handy tool called the **fossil record,** which assists them as they track changes in life-forms through geologic time.

It's important to keep in mind that not every dead organism becomes a fossil. A number of variables must all occur together. Perhaps the most important factor is the rapid burial of the organism's remains by sediments, sand, or ash, so that they are protected from decay and scavengers. Additionally, the fossil is a record biased toward organisms with hard parts—bones, teeth, and shells for example. They have a much higher probability of being preserved than soft-bodied organisms. Therefore, the fossil record is an incomplete record of evolutionary changes. Scientists work with the materials on hand to track evolutionary trends and infer phylogenetic relationships.

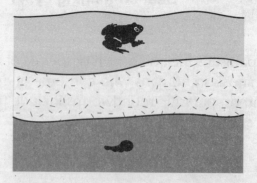

RATE OF EVOLUTION: GRADUALISM VS. PUNCTUATED EQUILIBRIUM

Until the 1970s, most scientists bought into the Darwinian model of evolution of **gradualism.** According to this model, fossil evidence suggests that evolution is a slow, gradual, and continuous process in which species change over long periods of time. This model is supported by the presence in the fossil record of species that change slightly from one rock layer to the next. In the 1970s, two scientists, **Stephen Jay Gould** and **Niles Eldridge,** proposed a new model for the evolution of species. The **punctuated equilibrium** model is characterized not by slow, gradual change accumulated over time, but rather by long periods of **stasis**—little or no physical changes—followed by short periods punctuated by abrupt physiological change in species. Scientists theorize that these abrupt changes result as a function of changing environmental pressures. During these periods of change, new species appeared in the fossil record while other species disappeared or became **extinct.**

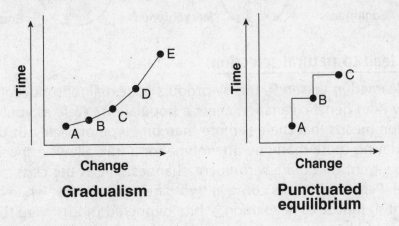

POPULATIONS CHANGE THROUGH TIME

The old children's song "The Old Gray Mare" says, "she ain't what she used to be." The fossil record agrees. It suggests that many groups of organisms, including horses, have undergone significant physiological changes throughout the course of geologic time. The fossil record provides a tool for tracking trends—directional changes in the characteristic features or patterns of diversity in a group of organisms—in the evolution of groups of organisms, including the well-studied trends in the evolution of horses.

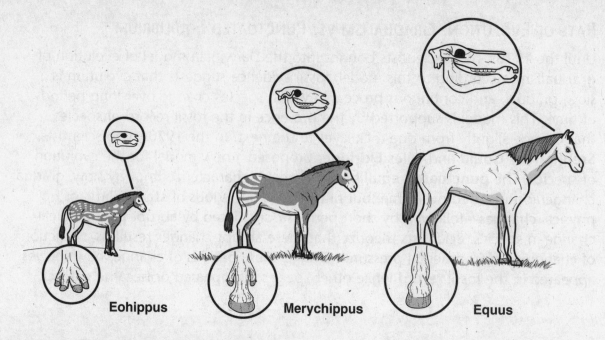

Eohippus   Merychippus   Equus

Adaptations lead to natural selection

Okay, as you learned in Lesson 9, the by-product of sexual reproduction is genetic variation. How does genetic variation affect a population? Well, as you've learned, genetic variation means that there is more than one type of allele out there for a given trait. Having more than one phenotype for a trait allows a species some flexibility in the event that the environment changes. This is the classic peppered moth example. Peppered moths come in two different varieties, white and black. Prior to the British Industrial Revolution, white peppered moths were the dominant phenotype over black peppered moths. As a result of the Industrial Revolution, soot and other pollutants were mixed into the air, creating a dark backdrop. This allowed the black moth population to benefit because the predatory pressure changed, making white moths easier targets than black moths. The population was able to adapt to an environmental change because it had a phenotype (black) within the population that was adaptable to the new environment.

A more current version of the peppered moth story is taking place today in medicine. Antibiotics are routinely prescribed to fight many bacterial infections. Although antibiotics kill most bacteria, antibiotic resistant organisms survive antibiotic treatment and go on to produce more antibiotic resistant bacteria. The antibiotic becomes the agent of selection for antibiotic resistance.

As a result of natural selection in sexually reproducing populations, gene frequency as indicated by the number of individuals of a given phenotype may be either increasing, decreasing, or remaining constant. Gene frequency is dependent upon the survival value and selective advantage that a phenotype imparts to organisms in a changing environment.

THE EMERGENCE OF NEW SPECIES

Speciation—the process by which genetically distinct species arise—results from the accumulation of adaptations over time. A biological **species** is defined as a population of organisms that can and does interbreed under natural environmental conditions producing fertile offspring. Hybrids are offspring produced from cross-species matings. In a few cases, such as a cross between a wolf and a dog, fertile offspring are produced even though parent organisms are from different species. More often cross-species matings result in **sterile** offspring. Isolating mechanisms that lead to speciation include geographic and reproductive isolation.

Geographic isolation

Geographic isolation refers to the physical separation of species populations by geographic barriers. Mountains, oceans, and canyons are examples of large-scale geographic barriers that effectively isolate one population from another. The earth's surface is dynamic. Mountains are uplifted and erode into hills over time. Oceans open and close. Volcanoes can rise up rapidly in a relatively short (geologically speaking) period of time. Crustal events such as these often produce environmental changes in the region of the event. Not only does a population become divided, but one of the segregated populations will also have to adapt to new environmental conditions. Thus, geographic isolation of a small population results in changes in gene frequency as well as selection for adaptations that make the species well suited for the new environment. Over time, different environmental conditions and different selective pressures result in the production of two genetically distinct populations.

Reproductive isolation

Species that are reproductively isolated from each other have the following qualities:
- Their reproductive organs are incompatible.
- They are genetically incompatible due to differences in chromosome number or genetic composition.
- Their gamete production takes place at different times of the day, month, or year.
- They do not recognize courtship behavior of other species.

LESSON 13
ECOLOGY

ECOLOGY

Ecology is the study of the interactions of living organisms with one another and with their physical environment. A **population** is a group of organisms that belong to the same species and inhabit a given geographic location at a given time. All the populations of different species living together in a given location at a given time form an ecological **community**. An **ecosystem** is how an ecological community interacts with the nonliving environment in which it is found. The **biosphere** is the portion of Earth in which living things exist.

DYNAMIC EQUILIBRIUM

Each population is a system that has its own dynamics and interrelationships. **Dynamic equilibrium** is achieved when the number of births in a population is equal to the number of deaths and when the number of individuals moving into a population (immigrating) is equal to the number of individuals leaving a population. This population is in dynamic equilibrium, because although the numbers remain the same (equilibrium), the actual faces making up the population change. If populations were allowed to increase unchecked, the population would increase exponentially. This condition occurs when birth and immigration rates dramatically exceed death and migration rates.

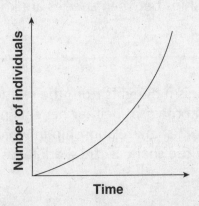

Most environments cannot support exponential population growth. A **logistic growth** curve represents a far more common pattern of population growth. In this pattern of restricted growth, populations may begin increasing exponentially, but growth rate soon slows as population density approaches the **carrying capacity** of the environment. Carrying capacity is the maximum number of individuals of a species that a given geographic region can support indefinitely.

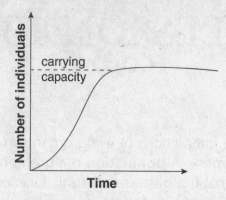

As a population approaches carrying capacity, death rate equals birthrate, achieving dynamic equilibrium such that there is no net increase in population size. So, what keeps these two rates in check? Abiotic and biotic **limiting factors.**

Abiotic limiting factors are nonliving environmental factors that affect a population regardless of its size. Oxygen concentration, moisture availability, and weather conditions—temperature range, snowstorms, floods, drought and so forth—affect all the individuals within a population. **Biotic** limiting factors are environmental factors that result from population interactions within the population (**intraspecific**) or with other populations (**interspecific**) within the ecosystem. **Biotic** limiting factors include intraspecific and interspecific competition for resources, such as food, water, minerals, or light, **predation**, and **parasitism.**

Population interactions

Symbiosis is the interrelationship between organisms that share an ecosystem. The three symbiotic relationships between species are known as commensalism, mutualism, and parasitism.

Commensalism

In **commensalism,** one organism benefits from the relationship with a member of a different species. The second organism neither benefits nor is harmed. An example of commensalism is the remora-shark relationship in which the remora benefits from the food scraps produced by the shark as the shark feeds.

Mutualism

Mutualism results in benefits for both interacting organisms. For example, a **lichen** is a mutualistic relationship between a fungus and an alga in which the fungus provides the alga with protection, and the alga provides the fungus with food from photosynthesis. Humans and *Escherichia coli* bacteria have a similar mutualistic relationship. Humans provide *E. coli* bacteria with protection while *E. coli* located in your intestines assist in the process of digestion.

Parasitism

Parasitism is a relationship in which one organism benefits at the expense of another. Mosquitoes, fleas, and ticks are external parasites that feed on living organisms and may introduce disease as they feed.

Nutrient cycling and energy flow through ecosystems

It's important to take a look at the big picture of nutrient cycling and energy flow through an ecosystem. Nutrient cycling provides organisms with elements and compounds essential to growth and development.

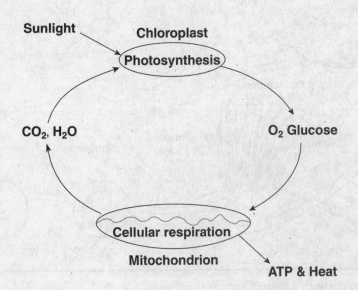

Nitrogen

Nitrogen is integral to the construction of nucleic and amino acids. Because all life on Earth contains nucleic and amino acids, nitrogen cycling plays a critical role in the continuation of life. Decomposers, such as fungi and bacteria (especially nitrogen-fixing bacteria), are essential to converting nitrogen-containing compounds to forms that are accessible to plants. Animals incorporate nitrogen absorbed from plants during consumption into their own tissues through digestion.

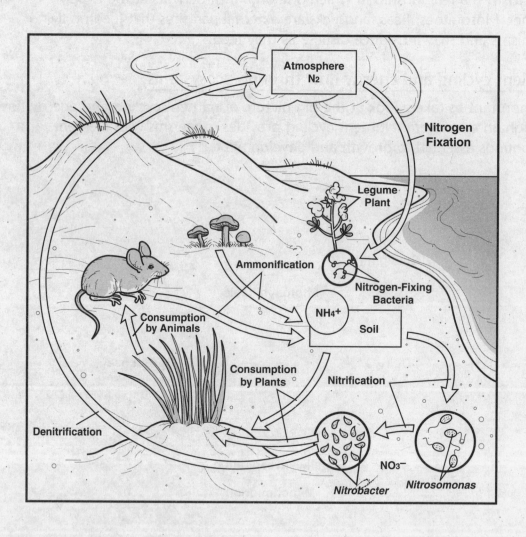

Water

Water is essential to all life on Earth. Both abiotic and biotic factors interact as water is transformed from one phase to another during the **water cycle.** As you've read earlier, water functions as a reactant, product, and solvent and is critical to homeostasis in most living organisms.

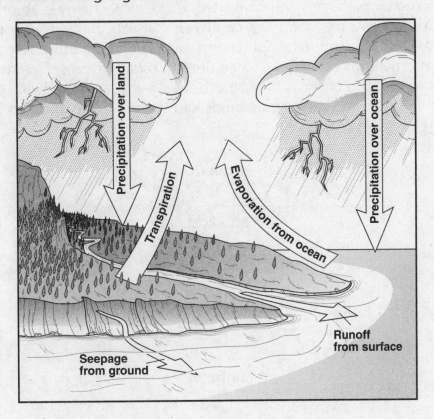

Energy

All processes and reactions carried out by living things require energy. Energy enters an ecosystem as solar energy absorbed by autotrophic organisms, such as plants and algae. Autotrophic organisms are the **producers** that convert solar energy into a form accessible to heterotrophic organisms, such as protists, fungi, and animals. Heterotrophic organisms ingest producers, thereby transferring energy from the producers to the **consumers. Decomposers,** such as fungi and bacteria, obtain energy from both producers and consumers after these organisms die.

A **food chain** is a linear transfer of energy through the ecosystem from a producer to a final consumer. The food chain always begins with energy from the Sun. This energy is absorbed by an autotroph or a green plant and is converted to chemical bond energy through the process of photosynthesis. Each link in the food chain is an organism that incorporates the energy absorbed by the organism that it consumes. Energy absorbed by producers and converted to chemical energy is absorbed by the **herbivore** that eats the plant. The **carnivore** that eats the herbivore absorbs the energy in the herbivore and the plant. Energy will continue to move through the food chain as organisms eat and are eaten until an organism dies. Decomposers are the final link in the food chain as they absorb the energy associated with organic compounds and release organic compounds into the soil to be absorbed by plants when the cycles begin again.

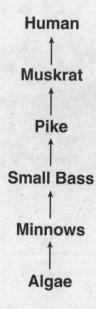

Human

↑

Muskrat

↑

Pike

↑

Small Bass

↑

Minnows

↑

Algae

A **food web** is the complex interaction of a number of food chains within an ecosystem.

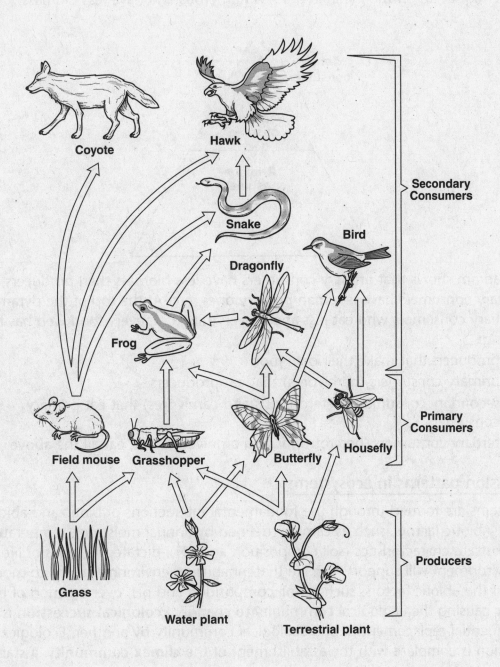

Coyote

Hawk

Snake

Bird

Dragonfly

Frog

Field mouse   Grasshopper   Butterfly   Housefly

Grass

Water plant

Terrestrial plant

Secondary Consumers

Primary Consumers

Producers

The energy flow, biomass (the total mass of all the organisms in an area), and population size within an ecosystem can be represented in a pyramid. Organisms that are higher up on the pyramid are less numerous and have less biomass.

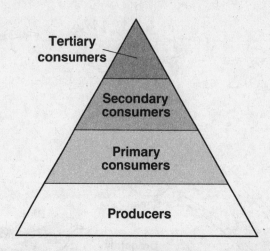

This diagram shows that primary consumers have less biomass than producers, and secondary consumers have less than primary ones, etc. At the top of the pyramid are the tertiary consumers who eat just about everything. So, every food web has the following:

- producers that make their own food
- primary consumers (herbivores) that eat producers
- secondary consumers (heterotrophs and carnivores) that eat primary consumers
- tertiary consumers (heterotrophs and omnivores) that eat all the above

Succession patterns in ecosystems

Ecosystems are formed through the fundamental interactions of biotic and abiotic factors. Abiotic factors, such as climate (defined by annual moisture), temperature, and substrate characteristics (soil composition and pH), dictate the types of life the environment will support. The life that inhabits an environment acts to modify some of the abiotic factors, such as soil composition and pH, over a period of time, thereby causing the ecological community to change. **Ecological succession** is the sequential replacement of one ecological community by another. Ecological succession is complete with the establishment of the **climax community,** a stable, self-perpetuating community.

Steps in succession

Ecological succession often begins on bare rock. A lichen is a **pioneering species** that establishes itself on bare rock. Lichens secrete enzymes that break down the rock, liberating minerals from the rock. Liberated minerals mixed with organic matter form the first very immature soils. There are enough minerals and organic matter available to support seeds from grasses and other herbaceous plants. Plants in the area, even grasses, lure animals. Animals contribute organic matter to the developing soil. As the soil develops, it supports shrubs, which in turn draw in larger animals. As the soil continues to develop through the physical and chemical weathering action of larger plants and the addition of more organic matter, new species of both plants and animals move into and dominate the area until a climax community is established.

A typical series of succession stages in Virginia might be as follows:
- lichens
- mosses
- grasses
- shrubs
- coniferous woodlands
- deciduous woodlands

The effects of natural events and human influence on ecosystems

Succession is not always initiated on bare rock. Although this is the most common course of succession, ecological succession has to be restarted from time to time as the environment itself wipes the slate clean. Major environmental events, such as volcanic eruptions, forest fires, and tornadoes, often strip an area of vegetative life. Because the plants dictate the type of animal life an ecosystem will support, an environmental event that wipes out local plants restarts the succession clock at time zero. After a major environmental event, the first species to return to an area are the pioneering species. Succession proceeds from that point forward.

Where do humans stand?

Historically, humans have had a significant and often negative impact on the environment. Human impact on the environment has included the following:
- poor land-use management policies that led to overgrazing and overhunting
- exploitation of natural resources that led to contamination of some fresh water supplies and increases in the rates of threatened, endangered, and extinct species

- introduction of foreign species that increased interspecific competition for natural resources often resulting in reduction or elimination of a natural population from the ecosystem
- industrial practices that produced soil, water, and air pollution
- the use of toxic herbicides and pesticides that reduced the fitness of natural populations

Turning the page

Within the past few decades years, humans have begun to rethink environmental philosophies. New policies and laws aimed at conserving natural populations and resources include the following:
- human population control through education and environmental awareness programs
- laws, regulations, and technology reducing air, water, and soil pollution
- laws and regulations mandating cleanup of contaminated environmental sites
- policies and practices designed to preserve threatened and endangered species
- development of environmentally friendly alternatives to fertilizers, herbicides, and pesticides

The new millennium

Technological advances in the past have often spelled ecological disaster for ecosystems. An increased understanding of the interrelatedness of species and improved understanding of the tenuous balance of most ecosystems has heightened human awareness of the human role in the grand scheme of things. Hopefully, the policies and the technology of the twenty-first century will reflect that awareness and continue to concentrate on the environment.

REVIEW FOR LESSONS 11–13

Take a few moments to practice test-taking strategies for questions about taxonomy and ecology. The answers and explanations are on page 157.

1 The roots of a mistletoe plant absorb nutrients from living oak trees causing some damage to the tissues of the trees. This is an example of—

A mutualism

B commensalism

C parasitism

D saprophytism

2 Which of the following best constitute an ecosystem?

F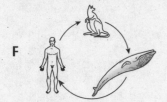

G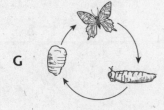

H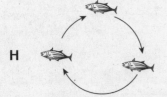

J

3 The diagram below represents a biomass pyramid.

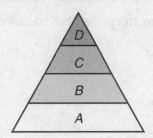

Which level of the pyramid most likely contains the greatest mass of herbivores?

A *A*

B *B*

C *C*

D *D*

4 If two different bird species in the same habitat require the same type of nesting site, both species will most likely—

F alternate the years that each species uses the nesting sites

G compete for the nesting sites

H share the same nesting sites

J change their nesting site requirements

5 A neighborhood birdfeeder is visited by a large number of seed-eating birds, such as chickadees, blue jays, cardinals, and finches. The birdfeeder is located at a home with a large number of different kinds of dogs, beagles, basset hounds, rottweilers, and German shepherds. Given the opportunity the dogs would interbreed. Why don't the birds interbreed?

    A Isolating mechanisms

    B Competition at the birdfeeder

    C The birds occupy different niches

    D The dogs belong to different species

ANSWERS AND EXPLANATIONS

1   **C   parasitism.** Here the mistletoe benefits at the oak tree's expense. Both the mistletoe and the oak tree must benefit for **A**, the mistletoe may benefit at no cost to the oak tree for **B**, and the mistletoe benefits at no cost to the oak tree because the oak tree is dead in **D**.

2   **J   a pond containing fish, plants, insects, and frogs. F** shows three different mammals. Each mammal lives in a different climate. **G** is the life cycle of a butterfly. **H** is three of the same kind of fish. **J** is a bunch of different organisms living in a pond. Therefore, **J** best represents an ecosystem.

3   **B   *B*.** The diagram represents a picture of the biomass pyramid where the greatest number of organisms, producers, are found at the bottom, **A**. Producers are green plants that convert solar energy into chemical energy, which is in turn absorbed by animals. Producers are consumed by primary consumers, on level *B* of the pyramid. Herbivores are primary consumers that feed on producers, so **B** is right.

4   **G   compete for the nesting sites.** May the best bird win. Competition between the species determines who gets a nesting site. **F, H**, and **J** are not valid.

5   **A   Isolating mechanisms.** Why don't the birds interbreed? The dogs all belong to the same species; but the birds belong to different species. **B**, competition for food, is not a barrier to interbreeding. **C** is not relevant to the question. Regardless of the breed of dog, all domestic dogs belong to the same species, so **D** is wrong.

THE PRACTICE TESTS

INSTRUCTIONS FOR TAKING THE PRACTICE TESTS

By this point, you've made it through the lesson sections of this book, covering all standards tested on the Virginia Standards of Learning (SOL) Biology Assessment. Congratulations! Now it's time to try your hand at a practice Biology SOL test. There are two in this section.

Each practice Biology SOL test includes sixty multiple-choice questions, just like the real test. Preceding each practice test is a bubble sheet. Tear or cut out this bubble sheet and answer your questions on the practice test by filling in the bubbles accordingly. Use a #2 pencil and take each practice test just as if you were taking the actual test. That means you should sit at a desk without a television or stereo on. It might help to turn off your phone, so you won't get disrupted.

The Biology SOL test is untimed, meaning you'll have as much time as you'll need to complete the test. However, you should still take the test in one sitting, because you won't be allowed to take a break during the real Biology SOL test. (However, you can go to the bathroom when you need to.)

Graphing calculators are allowed to be used during the Biology SOL test. Therefore, you should certainly take the practice SOL test with a calculator. You should get accustomed to working with your calculator. You will be allowed to use scratch paper, a ruler, and a compass.

When you've completed the first practice test, check the answers and explanations for it on page 177. Make sure to read through the explanations to all the questions—even the ones you got right. The explanations can help you figure out different ways to solve certain problems. After taking the first test and checking your answers, take a break. (Try not to take both practice tests in the same day—give your brain time to rest!) The answers and explanations for the second practice test can be found on page 203.

When you're ready, get started on Practice Test 1. (You'll have to cut out the bubble sheet too.) Good luck!

Practice Test 1

PRACTICE TEST 1 ANSWER SHEET

Name: _____

1. A B C D	21. A B C D	41. A B C D
2. F G H J	22. F G H J	42. F G H J
3. A B C D	23. A B C D	43. A B C D
4. F G H J	24. F G H J	44. F G H J
5. A B C D	25. A B C D	45. A B C D
6. F G H J	26. F G H J	46. F G H J
7. A B C D	27. A B C D	47. A B C D
8. F G H J	28. F G H J	48. F G H J
9. A B C D	29. A B C D	49. A B C D
10. F G H J	30. F G H J	50. F G H J
11. A B C D	31. A B C D	51. A B C D
12. F G H J	32. F G H J	52. F G H J
13. A B C D	33. A B C D	53. A B C D
14. F G H J	34. F G H J	54. F G H J
15. A B C D	35. A B C D	55. A B C D
16. F G H J	36. F G H J	56. F G H J
17. A B C D	37. A B C D	57. A B C D
18. F G H J	38. F G H J	58. F G H J
19. A B C D	39. A B C D	59. A B C D
20. F G H J	40. F G H J	60. F G H J

DIRECTIONS
Read each question carefully and choose the best answer. Then mark the space on the answer sheet for the answer you have chosen.

1 In humans, which organ is primarily responsible for the chemical digestion and absorption of food?

A Liver

B Stomach

C Small intestine

D Large intestine

2 Scientists find that the DNA sequences of Delmarva fox squirrels and cats are more similar than the sequences of fox squirrels and frogs. What do these findings suggest?

F Frogs are not related to fox squirrels.

G Fox squirrels are related more closely to cats than to frogs.

H Cats are more closely related to frogs than to fox squirrels.

J None of these animals are related.

3 Nutritional relationships between organisms are shown in the diagram below.

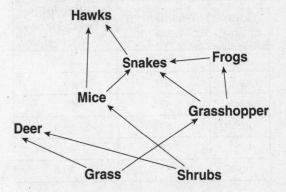

Which organisms are producers?

A Grass and shrubs

B Deer and mouse

C Grasshopper and frog

D Snake and hawk

4 What is the relationship between copperhead snakes and mice?

F Commensalism

G Mutualism

H Predator and prey

J Parasitism

5 The products of photosynthesis become the reactants in—

A dehydration synthesis

B the electron transport chain

C aerobic cellular respiration

D meiosis and mitosis

Base your answers to questions 6 through 8 on the information below and your knowledge of biology.

Color of light	Wavelength of light (nm)	% absorption by spinach extract
red	674	41.0
orange	616	32.1
yellow	585	25.8
green	533	17.8
blue	457	49.8
violet	412	49.8

6 Which graph accurately shows the relationship between wavelength and percent absorption?

F
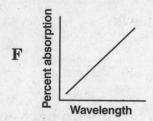

G
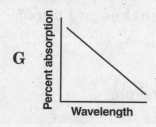

H
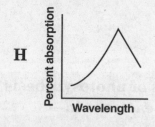

J
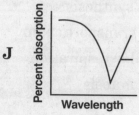

7 Which colored light has the longest wavelength?

A Red

B Orange

C Blue

D Violet

8 Which statement is a valid conclusion that can be drawn from the data obtained in this investigation?

F All plants absorb green and yellow lights equally.

G Photosynthetic pigments in spinach plants absorb blue light more efficiently than they absorb red light.

H Photosynthetic pigments in spinach plants absorb green light more efficiently than they absorb orange light.

J The data would be the same for all pigments in spinach leaves.

9 Which organism has a transport system most similar to that of the earthworm?

A Oak tree

B Sponge

C Human

D Bacterium

10 Malaria is a disease caused by *Plasmodium* bacteria and spread by mosquitoes of the genus *Anopheles*. Why have efforts to eliminate malaria *not* been successful?

F Resistant strains of mosquitoes and *Plasmodium* have evolved.

G Spraying programs have been inconsistent.

H The symptoms of malaria are easily confused with those of other diseases.

J The life cycle of *Anopheles* is not well understood.

11 When a test tube of water containing *elodea* (an aquatic plant) is placed near a white light, the plant gives off gas bubbles. When *elodea* is placed near different colors of light, the rate of bubbling is affected. The experimental variable in this demonstration is the—

A type of plant used

B distance of plant from light source

C color of light source

D temperature of water in test tube

12 Which part of the blood is correctly paired with its function?

F Red blood cells—transport wastes

G White blood cells—fight infection

H Plasma—produce antibodies

J Platelets—transport hormones

13 Which structures could most likely be observed in cells in the low-power field of a compound light microscope?

A Genes and cell walls

B Vacuoles and nucleotides

C Proteins and ribosomes

D Chloroplasts and nuclei

14 Osmosis is a type of—

F active transport

G passive transport

H facilitated diffusion

J ion transport

15 Which two environmental variables determine the type of climax vegetation associated with a terrestrial biome?

A Air pressure and wind speed

B Temperature and moisture

C Cloud cover and temperature

D Wind direction and elevation

16 During anaerobic respiration, pyruvic acid is converted to—

   F water

   G carbon dioxide

   H cellulose

   J lactic acid

17 Which substance is a suitable indicator for detecting starch in a plant cell?

   A Saline solution

   B Biuret solution

   C Iodine solution

   D Sudan solution

18 In the diagram of a cell, which number indicates the structure in which most of the enzymes involved in aerobic cellular respiration function?

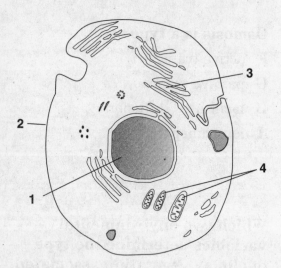

   F 1

   G 2

   H 3

   J 4

19 Which organism obtains nutrients from other organisms by extracellular digestion and absorption?

   A Mushroom

   B Oak tree

   C Rose bush

   D Sponge

20 Gould and Eldridge observed that organisms in the fossil record remained unchanged for long periods of time followed by short periods of rapid change. These observations led them to develop the theory of—

   F gradualism

   G dynamic equilibrium

   H natural selection

   J punctuated equilibrium

21 Which factor promotes competition in an ecosystem?

   A A high number of predators

   B Limited resources

   C Several different types of niches

   D Nutrient cycling

22 A new drug for the treatment of hypertension is tested on five hundred people. The people are divided into two groups. Members of group X receive a glucose pill. Members of group Y receive the drug. Group X serves as the—

   F control group

   G experimental group

   H variable group

   J conditional group

23 A microscope with a 4x objective lens and a 10x ocular lens produces a total magnification of—

   A 14x

   B 40x

   C 400x

   D 4000x

24 Proteins are formed by bonding amino acids together through the process of—

   F cellular respiration

   G dehydration synthesis

   H hydrolysis

   J ionization

25 A study was conducted using two groups of ten plants of the same species. During the study, the plants were placed in identical environmental conditions. The plants in one group were given a growth solution every three days. The heights of the plants in both groups were recorded at the beginning of the study and at the end of a three-week period. The data showed that the plants given the growth solution grew faster than those not given the solution. When other researchers conduct this study to test the accuracy of the results, they should—

   A not give growth solution to both groups

   B change the light levels for both groups

   C double the amount of growth solution given to the first group

   D keep conditions identical to the first study

26 What causes the stem of a bean plant to bend toward the light?

   F Gravity

   G Starch deposits

   H Water

   J Auxin distribution

27 Which process does the diagram below illustrate?

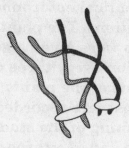

A Crossing-over

B Nondisjunction

C Sex determination

D Independent assortment

28 Which activity is represented by the arrows in the diagram below?

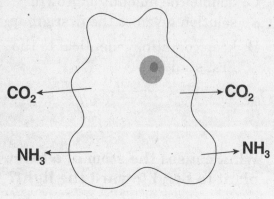

F Autotrophic nutrition

G Anaerobic respiration

H Dehydration synthesis

J Excretion of wastes

29 What are the structures specialized for taking blood away from the heart called?

A Capillaries

B Arteries

C Bronchioles

D Veins

30 Which statement best describes the technique known as karyotyping?

F Some of the fluid surrounding the fetus is removed for analysis.

G Photographs of chromosomes are developed, cut up, and arranged in homologous pairs.

H DNA from different organisms are spliced together to produce recombinant DNA.

J Organisms are separated into groups based on physical and molecular characteristics.

31 The ability of water to absorb and release heat energy is important for the maintenance of—

A metabolism

B photosynthesis

C cellular respiration

D homeostasis

32 What is the first step of a scientific investigation?

F Formulate a hypothesis

G Gather and analyze data

H Identify a question

J Design an experiment

33 Use the table below to answer the question that follows.

Enzyme	Effective temp. range (°C)	Optimum pH
1	37–42	7.2
2	30–37	2.0
3	20–30	9.0
4	20–27	3.5

Which enzyme would most likely denature at 35°C?

A 1

B 2

C 3

D 4

34 Two organisms are represented in the diagram below.

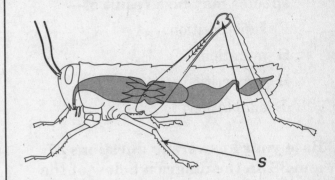

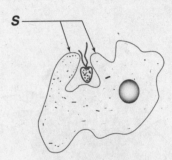

The arrows in the diagram indicate structures (S) that help these organisms—

F reproduce

G carry out respiration

H obtain food

J carry out photosynthesis

35 Carbohydrates are stored in the liver and muscles of animals in the form of—

A glucose

B glycerol

C glycogen

D glycine

36 A change in genetic material that produces a variation in a species may be a result of—

F superposition

G mutation

H competition

J adaptation

Base your answers to questions 37 and 38 on the diagram below of the human heart and your knowledge of biology.

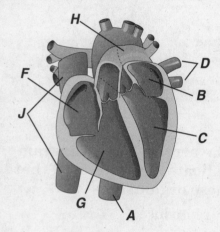

37 Which structure pumps blood into the aorta?

A *A*

B *B*

C *C*

D *D*

38 Which structure transports deoxygenated blood back to the lungs?

F *F*

G *G*

H *H*

J *J*

39 An increase in the number of cells is the result of—

A fertilization

B gastrulation

C differentiation

D growth

40 Based on experimental results, a biologist in a laboratory reports a new discovery. If the experimental results are valid, biologists in other laboratories should be able to perform—

F a different experiment to produce the same results

G a different experiment to produce different results

H the same experiment to produce the same results

J the same experiment to produce different results

41 What do you call the molecules that function in the short-term relay of information from cell to cell?

A Neurotransmitters

B Hormones

C Chemical messengers

D Neurons

42 In order to preserve the biosphere for future generations, humans must—

F introduce new species into an ecosystem

G develop species survival plans for all species in an ecosystem

H understand how living things interact within their environment

J alter the environment to meet the needs of endangered species

43 Reactions in anaerobic and aerobic respiration are controlled by—

A enzymes

B oxygen

C pyruvic acid

D water

44 Which scientist determined that new cells arise from preexisting cells?

F Darwin

G Virchow

H Mendel

J Schleiden

45 The diagram below shows the gradual change over time in the anatomy of the horse.

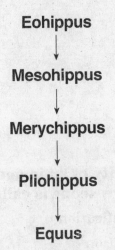

Which concept best explains the physical change in horse structure and size over geologic time?

A Artificial selection

B Codominance

C Organic evolution

D Karyotype

46 Which process is a form of autotrophic nutrition?

F Cellular digestion

G Photosynthesis

H Fermentation

J Regulation

47 An enzyme that works best in an alkaline environment would function best at a pH of—

A 9

B 7

C 5

D 3

48 The clarity of an image produced by a microscope is called—

F magnification

G resolution

H micrograph

J amplification

49 In many breeds of cattle, the polled condition (absence of horns) is dominant over the presence of horns, and homozygous red coat color crossed with homozygous white coat color produces roan (the presence of both white and red hairs). Which cross will produce only horned roan offspring?

A Polled red X horned white

B Horned roan X horned roan

C Horned red X horned white

D Polled roan X horned roan

50 Which macromolecule contains nitrogen?

F Protein

G Carbohydrate

H Lipid

J Water

51 Which components of DNA are held together by weak hydrogen bonds?

A Adenine and thymine

B Cytosine and phosphate

C Deoxyribose and guanine

D Phosphate and deoxyribose

52 The volume of the liquid in the graduated cylinder shown below is—

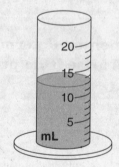

F 11.0 mL

G 12.0 mL

H 12.5 mL

J 13.0 mL

53 Membrane proteins that aid in the active transport of materials into and out of the cell are called—

A signal proteins

B marker proteins

C receptor proteins

D transport proteins

54 Viruses are exceptions to the cell theory. However, they do share some characteristics with living things. What is one characteristic that viruses share with living things?

F They contain chloroplasts.

G They reproduce through mitosis.

H They contain genetic material.

J They contain membrane-bound organelles.

55 The first eukaryotic kingdom was the kingdom—

A Animalia

B Plantae

C Protista

D *Eubacteria*

56 Which reproductive adaptation is characteristic of most terrestrial vertebrates?

F External fertilization

G Internal fertilization

H External development

J Short gestational period

57 The energy that drives metabolism in animals is derived from—

A homeostasis

B food

C water

D heredity

58 A chemical analysis of organisms from each kingdom shows that living things are primarily composed of the elements—

F carbon, hydrogen, nitrogen, and oxygen

G zinc, magnesium, carbon, and hydrogen

H iron, sulfur, oxygen, and hydrogen

J chlorine, calcium, carbon, and lead

59 A factor that affects an enzyme's ability to work efficiently is—

A size

B shape

C source

D sequence

60 Aphids are small sucking insects that feed on the sap of plants. Honeydew is a sap that is secreted by aphids and is a food source for ants. Ants provide aphids with protection against predators. The relationship that exists between aphids and ants is known as—

F parasitism

G commensalism

H mutualism

J saprophytism

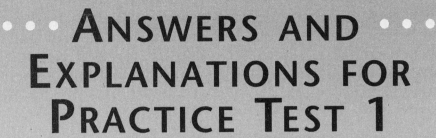

ANSWERS AND EXPLANATIONS FOR PRACTICE TEST 1

PRACTICE TEST 1: ANSWERS AND EXPLANATIONS

1   **C**   The liver, **A**, contributes digestive enzymes, but is not the site of digestion and absorption. The mechanical and chemical breakdown of food that was begun in the mouth continues in the stomach. However, very little nutrients are absorbed in the stomach, so **B** is wrong. The bulk of digestion takes place in the small intestine, **C**. The large intestine, **D**, acts like a solid-waste packaging site.

2   **G**   Similarities in DNA sequences are used to infer species relatedness. The more similar the sequences, the more closely related the species are inferred to be. Because fox squirrels and cats have a greater similarity between genetic sequences than fox squirrels and frogs do, you may infer that it has been a longer period of time since fox squirrels and frogs shared a common ancestor than when fox squirrels and cats shared a common ancestor.

3   **A**   Autotrophic organisms, such as grass and shrubs, are the producers in a food web. They convert solar energy to chemical energy that then becomes available to primary consumers, herbivores, in the community. Secondary consumers, such as frogs, snakes, and hawks, consume primary consumers.

4   **H**   Virginia's copperheads are predators of mice, lizards, amphibians, birds, and other snakes.

5   **C**   Oxygen and carbohydrates produced by photosynthesis become the reactants in aerobic cellular respiration. Dehydration synthesis, **A**, is a process necessary for the production of such polymers as starch and polypeptides. The electron transport chain, **B**, is integral to the transfer of energy leading to the formation of ATP. Meiosis and mitosis, **D**, are types of cell division that require energy but are not directly linked to either photosynthesis or aerobic cellular respiration.

6   **J**   The data indicate that percent absorption is highest at short wavelengths. As wavelength increases, percent absorption decreases, rapidly bottoming out at the green colored light. Beyond this wavelength, percent absorption again increases.

7   **A**   Red light comes in with the longest wavelength at 674 nanometers. Violet light has the shortest wavelength at 412 nanometers.

8   **G**   The data indicate that blue light is absorbed more efficiently (approximately 50%) than red light is (41%). Green light has the lowest absorption at approximately 18%, almost half as efficient as orange light at 32%, making **F** and **H** untrue. **J** is untrue, because different pigments absorb wavelengths at different rates.

9　**C**　Humans have transport systems most similar to those of earthworms. Both humans and earthworms have closed circulatory systems that transport dissolved gases and nutrients throughout each organ. The vascular system of an oak tree, **A**, is very different from that of an earthworm. Sponges, **B**, and bacteria, **D**, lack vascular systems.

10　**F**　Mosquitoes are sexually reproducing organisms that produce a very large number of offspring. This condition sets the stage for the probability that mosquitoes with resistance to the insecticide survive spraying campaigns, resulting in the evolution of insecticide-resistant populations of *Plasmodium*-carrying mosquitoes and the perpetuation of malaria.

11　**C**　In this experiment, light color changed from white to colored. The type of plant, **A**, remains the same as does the distance of the plant from the light source, **B**. Temperature, **D**, was not mentioned and therefore is inferred to have remained the same.

12　**G**　White blood cells perform many immune functions, among them fighting infections by producing antibodies. Red blood cells, **F**, carry oxygen. Plasma, **H**, is the liquid portion of the blood that transports wastes and hormones. Platelets, **J**, play an important role in wound-healing by releasing proteins and clotting factors at the site of an injury.

13　**D**　Under the low-power field of a compound light microscope, **D** provides the only correct combination of organelles and structures large enough to be visible; genes, nucleotides, proteins, and ribosomes are too small to be visible.

14　**G**　Osmosis is a form of passive transport. No energy is spent as material water passes through the cell membrane into the cell along the concentration gradient. Active transport, **F**, requires the addition of energy as does facilitated diffusion, **H**. Ions are transported, **J**, into and out of a cell by sodium/potassium pumps and hydrogen pumps. All ion transports require energy.

15　**B**　Annual temperature and moisture are two important variables that affect the tyonal temperature. High elevations experience lower annual temperatures than locations at sea level.

16　**J**　Anaerobic respiration is cellular respiration that takes place in the absence of oxygen. During lactic acid fermentation, lactic acid is produced in addition to ATP. The other type of fermentation, alcoholic fermentation, results in the production of ethyl alcohol and carbon dioxide in addition to ATP.

17　**C**　Iodine solution (Lugol's) is a common indicator used to detect the presence of starch. Biuret solution, **B**, is used to detect protein. Sudan solution, **D**, is used to detect fats. Saline solution, **A**, is not an indicator.

18   **J**   Structure 4 is a mitochondrion. Mitochondria contain enzymes that function in aerobic cellular respiration. Structure 1 is the nucleus, which contains DNA, the genetic material of the cell. Structure 2 is the cell membrane, which regulates the material that moves into and out of the cell. Structure 3 is the endoplasmic reticulum, which transports lipids and proteins around the interior of the cell.

19   **A**   Mushrooms, like most heterotrophic members of this phylum, are decomposers that secrete enzymes as a means of breaking down organic materials. Organic molecules are then absorbed. Sponges, **D**, are heterotrophic organisms that carry out intracellular digestion. Oak trees, **B**, and rose bushes, **C**, are autotrophic and therefore generate their own organic molecules.

20   **J**   The evolutionary theory of punctuated equilibrium states that organisms remain unchanged for long periods of time followed by brief periods of rapid change. Species extinction may result from inability to adapt to changing environmental conditions. Gradualism, **F**, is the evolutionary theory proposed by Darwin stating that organisms change gradually over time. Dynamic equilibrium, **G**, is achieved when the number of births in a population is equal to the number of deaths. Natural selection, **H**, is the mechanism that Darwin proposed for the evolution of species.

21   **B**   Competition within and between species increases as resource availability decreases within an ecosystem. A high number of predators, **A**, may or may not increase competition, particularly if the prey of these predators are different. Snakes, hawks, and mountain lions may all be predators in an ecosystem without being in competition with each other for the same types of prey. Animals that occupy different niches, **C**, often do not come into competition with each other. Nutrient cycling, **D**, does not affect competition.

22   **F**   Group X serves as the control group against which the results of the experimental group Y are measured. Members of both groups are unaware of the treatment they are receiving. The variable in the experiment is the drug.

23   **B**   You determine the total magnification of the image viewed through a light microscope by *multiplying* the magnification of the objective lens times the magnification of the ocular lens.

24   **G**   Dehydration synthesis is the chemical combination of macromolecules resulting in the formation of larger macromolecules and the removal of one water molecule. Cellular respiration, **F**, is the biochemical process that results in the production of carbon dioxide, water, and ATP. Hydrolysis, **H**, breaks big macromolecules into their component parts through the addition of a water molecule. During ionization, **J**, a charged particle, an ion, is formed through the loss or gain of an electron.

25 **D** In order to validate the results of the first study and reproduce results similar to the first study, experimental conditions must be the same. Not administering growth solution, **A**, changing light levels, **B**, and doubling the amount of growth solution used, **C**, will produce results different from those of the original study.

26 **J** The bending of plants toward the light is phototropism. Phototropism results from unequal cell growth along the stem that is produced by unequal auxin distribution. Gravitropism causes roots and shoots of plants to grow in the directions that they do relative to the pull of gravity, **F**. Water, **H**, and starch deposits, **G**, do not influence the apparent bending of plants.

27 **A** The diagram illustrates a crossing-over process in which genetic material is exchanged between homologous chromosomes during meiosis. Crossing-over accounts for genetic variability in offspring within families. Nondisjunction, **B**, is the failure of homologous chromosomes to separate during the first phase of meiosis. Sex determination, **C**, occurs during fertilization. In humans, male offspring are the result of fertilization by sperm carrying a Y chromosome. Females are determined by sperm carrying an X chromosome. Independent assortment, **D**, is the random distribution of traits during cell division. Traits are inherited independently of each other.

28 **J** Carbon dioxide and ammonia are metabolic wastes that diffuse across the surface of *Amoeba*. None of the other processes (**F**, **G**, or **H**) are involved in excretion from a cell.

29 **B** Arteries are large blood vessels that carry blood away from the heart. Veins, **D**, are blood vessels that carry blood back to the heart. Capillaries, **A**, are the smallest blood vessels through which gases diffuse. Bronchioles, **C**, are one of several subdivisions of the bronchi found in the lungs.

30 **G** Karyotyping is the arrangement of photographic images of chromosomes into homologous pairs. During amniocentesis, **F**, amniotic fluid is removed and tested for genetic abnormalities. Recombinant DNA, **H**, is produced as a result of genetic engineering. Taxonomy, **J**, is the separation of organisms into groups based on physical and molecular similarities.

31 **D** The question asked about water's ability to absorb and release heat energy. This is a question about water's regulatory function. Homeostasis is the maintenance of internal temperature in addition to other conditions. Therefore, water acts to maintain internal temperature conditions. Water does play a vital molecular role in **A**, **B**, and **C**, but not a regulatory role.

32 **H** Of the choices provided, before any of the other steps can be carried out, a question must be identified. Formulating a hypothesis, **F**, then designing an experiment to test the hypothesis, **J**, and gathering and analyzing data, **G**, follow this initial step.

33   **D** Enzymes denature at temperatures well above their optimum range. When enzymes denature, the protein structure breaks down inhibiting function. At 35°C, enzyme 1 functions slightly less efficiently and enzyme 2 operates within its optimal range. At this temperature, enzyme 3 will function less efficiently. Enzymatic activity will more than likely cease at eight degrees beyond its maximum.

34   **H** The legs of a grasshopper and the pseudopodia of *Amoeba* are instrumental in helping these organisms obtain food. Both organisms are heterotrophic and therefore neither carries out photosynthesis, **J**. Grasshoppers reproduce sexually using specialized structures. *Amoeba* reproduce asexually through binary fission. So, **F** is incorrect.

35   **C** Glycogen is the short-term storage form of carbohydrates found in the liver and muscles of animals. Glucose, **A**, is the monosaccharide used in cellular respiration. Glycerol, **B**, is an organic compound associated with lipids. Glycine, **D**, is one of twenty amino acids.

36   **G** Insertions, deletions, and substitutions are mutations that may result in genetic change and therefore genetic variation. Superposition, **F**, is the order of rock layers in an undisturbed rock column. The principle of superposition is used to determine the relative age of fossil organisms found in the rock column. Competition, **H**, does not directly influence the genetic composition of organisms, but may act as an agent of selection. Adaptation, **J**, includes any phenotypic characteristics available at low frequencies that may become more important or increase species survival in the event of environment change.

37   **C** The left ventricle pumps blood into the aorta, **A**, where the blood is then transported to all parts of the body. **B** is the left atrium which receives oxygenated blood from the pulmonary veins, **D**. The left atrium sends oxygenated blood into the left ventricle through valves that prevent blood from flowing back into the atrium.

38   **H** The pulmonary artery is the only artery that transports deoxygenated blood from the heart to the lungs. The right atrium, **F**, receives deoxygenated blood from the vena cava, **J**, and pumps this deoxygenated blood into the right ventricle, **G**. Blood from the right ventricle is pumped into the pulmonary artery where it is returned to the lungs for reoxygenation.

39   **D** Growth results in an increase in the number of cells and cell size. An elephant's cells are not necessarily larger than the cells of a mouse. An elephant simply has more cells.

40　**H**　To test the validity of any scientific discovery, the same experiment should be performed under the same experimental conditions. The results of the first experiment are validated if the results of the second experiment are identical to the results of the first. Different experiments, **F** and **G**, cannot be used to validate the experimental results of the first experiment. If the same experiment is performed with different results, **J**, then the original experiment has not been validated, requiring further inquiry.

41　**A**　This one could definitely be a toughie if you don't have your understanding of cell communication straight. Neurotransmitters are messenger molecules produced by nerve cells or neurons, **D**. Neurotransmitters operate for short terms and move from one nerve cell to the next. On the other hand, hormones, **B**, are chemical messengers, **C**, that perform in a more long-term communication role. Hormones are produced in one location but function in another.

42　**H**　To better preserve the biosphere in the future, it is important that humans understand the interaction between species within their environment. The introduction of alien species, **F**, has been responsible for the downfall of many indigenous species. Species survival plans, **G**, are management plans designed to preserve endangered species. Any change in the environment, **J**, will upset the balance of the ecosystem.

43　**A**　Enzymes are the be-all and end-all regulatory molecules of biochemical reactions, including those involved in both anaerobic and aerobic respiration.

44　**G**　Rudolf von Virchow determined that cells were not the result of spontaneous generation but rather arose from preexisting cells. Darwin, **F**, is credited with developing the theory of natural selection. Mendel, **H**, is credited with founding modern genetics. Schleiden, **J**, determined that plants are composed of cells.

45　**C**　Changes in the anatomical structures and size of the horse over geologic time have been attributed to organic evolution. Artificial selection, **A**, is used in animal husbandry and agriculture to select for specific traits, such as milk production and fruit size or sweetness. Codominance, **B**, is the expression of both alleles for a given trait. Karyotype, **D**, is the map of homologous chromosomes that illustrates the number and length of chromosomes in the nucleus of body cells.

46　**G**　Autotrophic organisms are those organisms that carry out photosynthesis in order to obtain nutrients. Cellular digestion, **F**, is carried out by heterotrophic protists and eukaryotic organisms (sponges, for example) without specific digestive organs or compartments. Fermentation, **H**, is a form of anaerobic cellular respiration. Regulation, **J**, involves a number of systems and molecules aimed at maintaining homeostasis.

47   **A**   Alkaline environments have pH values greater than 7. A pH equal to 7 is a neutral solution that is neither alkaline nor acidic. Values below 7 indicate acidic conditions.

48   **G**   The clarity of the image produced by a microscope refers to the resolution of the image. Magnification increases the size of the image as does amplification. A micrograph is the image produced by an electron microscope.

49   **C**   The question told you that horns are a homozygous recessive condition. Therefore, both parents must be homozygous recessive for horns to appear in all offspring. This eliminates **A** and **D** from consideration. Roan coat color is a result of codominant expression, which is genotypically heterozygous. To produce all roan offspring, both parents must be homozygous for coat color. This eliminates **B.** Crossing roan parents would produce red, roan, or white offspring.

50   **F**   Of the macromolecules listed, protein is the only one that contains nitrogen. Carbohydrates, **G**, and lipids, **H**, are hydrocarbons that do not include nitrogen in their structural formulas. Water, **J**, is not a macromolecule.

51   **A**   In a molecule of DNA, base pairs, adenine and thymine as well as cytosine and guanine, are held together by weak hydrogen bonds. Cytosine is bonded to deoxyribose, not phosphate, so **B** is incorrect. Both **C** and **D** represent molecular combinations held together by covalent bonds.

52   **G**   The volume of the liquid is 12.0 when read at the bottom of the meniscus, the curve at the top of the liquid.

53   **D**   Transport proteins act as channels through which molecules and ions move against the concentration gradient. Signal proteins, **A**, are molecules received at the surface of the cell by receptor proteins, **C**, which may initiate the formation of a secondary signal molecule inside the cell. Marker proteins, **B**, are proteins on the surface of the cell that identify the cell.

54   **H**   Viruses contain short segments of nucleic acids. They do not reproduce through mitosis, **G**. Instead, viruses reproduce by infecting other cells. Viral DNA is incorporated into the DNA of the host cell, which then reproduces the viral DNA when it reproduces its own. Viruses do not contain membrane-bound organelles, **J**, including chloroplasts, **F**.

55   **C**   The evolution of protists and the kingdom Protista represents the first appearance of eukaryotic cells about 1,500 million years ago. Simple animals, **A**, and primitive plants, **B**, show up in the rock record about one million years ago. *Eubacteria*, **D**, are prokaryotes.

56　**G**　Terrestrial vertebrates are adapted for internal fertilization as a strategy for preventing gametes from drying out. After fertilization, development may be external (birds, most reptiles) or internal (mammals), so **H** is incorrect. External fertilization, **F,** is characteristic of amphibians and most aquatic vertebrates. Gestational period is the length of time from fertilization until hatching or birth. This period is species dependent, so **J** is incorrect.

57　**B**　Food obtained by animals through various means provides the energy needed to carry out metabolic and life processes. Homeostasis, **A,** is the maintenance of a constant internal environment. Water, **C,** is an important reagent in most biochemical reactions in addition to playing an important role in homeostasis. Heredity, **D,** is the passage of genetic information from one generation to the next.

58　**F**　Life's macromolecules are constructed primarily from the elements carbon, hydrogen, nitrogen, and oxygen. Zinc, calcium, magnesium, and iron are just a few trace elements necessary for biochemical reactions involved in metabolism.

59　**B**　The functionality of enzymes is most affected by each enzyme's shape. Enzyme size, **A,** does not affect function. Enzymes are proteins constructed on the surface of ribosomes and are all derived from the same source, so **C** is incorrect. Sequence, **D,** is a term applied to DNA.

60　**H**　Mutualism is a relationship between organisms in which both organisms benefit. Parasitism, **F,** results when one organism benefits at the expense of another. Commensalism, **G,** is the beneficial gain of one organism while the other organism remains unaffected. Saprophytism, **J,** is a form of heterotrophic nutrition in which an organism obtains nutrients from decaying organic matter. Decomposers such as fungi and bacteria are saprophytes.

PRACTICE TEST 2

PRACTICE TEST 2 ANSWER SHEET

Name: _____

1. Ⓐ Ⓑ Ⓒ Ⓓ   21. Ⓐ Ⓑ Ⓒ Ⓓ   41. Ⓐ Ⓑ Ⓒ Ⓓ

2. Ⓕ Ⓖ Ⓗ Ⓙ   22. Ⓕ Ⓖ Ⓗ Ⓙ   42. Ⓕ Ⓖ Ⓗ Ⓙ

3. Ⓐ Ⓑ Ⓒ Ⓓ   23. Ⓐ Ⓑ Ⓒ Ⓓ   43. Ⓐ Ⓑ Ⓒ Ⓓ

4. Ⓕ Ⓖ Ⓗ Ⓙ   24. Ⓕ Ⓖ Ⓗ Ⓙ   44. Ⓕ Ⓖ Ⓗ Ⓙ

5. Ⓐ Ⓑ Ⓒ Ⓓ   25. Ⓐ Ⓑ Ⓒ Ⓓ   45. Ⓐ Ⓑ Ⓒ Ⓓ

6. Ⓕ Ⓖ Ⓗ Ⓙ   26. Ⓕ Ⓖ Ⓗ Ⓙ   46. Ⓕ Ⓖ Ⓗ Ⓙ

7. Ⓐ Ⓑ Ⓒ Ⓓ   27. Ⓐ Ⓑ Ⓒ Ⓓ   47. Ⓐ Ⓑ Ⓒ Ⓓ

8. Ⓕ Ⓖ Ⓗ Ⓙ   28. Ⓕ Ⓖ Ⓗ Ⓙ   48. Ⓕ Ⓖ Ⓗ Ⓙ

9. Ⓐ Ⓑ Ⓒ Ⓓ   29. Ⓐ Ⓑ Ⓒ Ⓓ   49. Ⓐ Ⓑ Ⓒ Ⓓ

10. Ⓕ Ⓖ Ⓗ Ⓙ   30. Ⓕ Ⓖ Ⓗ Ⓙ   50. Ⓕ Ⓖ Ⓗ Ⓙ

11. Ⓐ Ⓑ Ⓒ Ⓓ   31. Ⓐ Ⓑ Ⓒ Ⓓ   51. Ⓐ Ⓑ Ⓒ Ⓓ

12. Ⓕ Ⓖ Ⓗ Ⓙ   32. Ⓕ Ⓖ Ⓗ Ⓙ   52. Ⓕ Ⓖ Ⓗ Ⓙ

13. Ⓐ Ⓑ Ⓒ Ⓓ   33. Ⓐ Ⓑ Ⓒ Ⓓ   53. Ⓐ Ⓑ Ⓒ Ⓓ

14. Ⓕ Ⓖ Ⓗ Ⓙ   34. Ⓕ Ⓖ Ⓗ Ⓙ   54. Ⓕ Ⓖ Ⓗ Ⓙ

15. Ⓐ Ⓑ Ⓒ Ⓓ   35. Ⓐ Ⓑ Ⓒ Ⓓ   55. Ⓐ Ⓑ Ⓒ Ⓓ

16. Ⓕ Ⓖ Ⓗ Ⓙ   36. Ⓕ Ⓖ Ⓗ Ⓙ   56. Ⓕ Ⓖ Ⓗ Ⓙ

17. Ⓐ Ⓑ Ⓒ Ⓓ   37. Ⓐ Ⓑ Ⓒ Ⓓ   57. Ⓐ Ⓑ Ⓒ Ⓓ

18. Ⓕ Ⓖ Ⓗ Ⓙ   38. Ⓕ Ⓖ Ⓗ Ⓙ   58. Ⓕ Ⓖ Ⓗ Ⓙ

19. Ⓐ Ⓑ Ⓒ Ⓓ   39. Ⓐ Ⓑ Ⓒ Ⓓ   59. Ⓐ Ⓑ Ⓒ Ⓓ

20. Ⓕ Ⓖ Ⓗ Ⓙ   40. Ⓕ Ⓖ Ⓗ Ⓙ   60. Ⓕ Ⓖ Ⓗ Ⓙ

Read each question carefully and choose the best answer. Then mark the space on the answer sheet for the answer you have chosen.

1 The large amount of salt in the air and water near the coastal area of Virginia determines which species can exist there. In these areas, the salt functions as a—

A limiting factor

B biotic factor

C reactant

D food source

2 Which pattern of evolution is characterized by long periods of stability interrupted by brief periods of significant physiological change?

F Punctuated equilibrium

G Dynamic equilibrium

H The climax community

J Homeostasis

3 In which process is the pairing of homologous chromosomes followed by the disjunction of these chromosome pairs?

A Fertilization

B Meiosis

C Budding

D Segregation

4 Hydra remove nitrogenous wastes from their cells mainly by—

F metabolism

G osmosis

H diffusion

J homeostasis

Base your answer to question 5 on the graph below and your understanding of biology. The graph illustrates the change in the pattern of yeast growth over time.

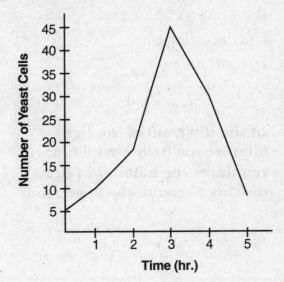

5 Approximately how many yeast cells were present after 3.5 hours?

A 20

B 25

C 30

D 35

6 Chitin is a structural molecule found in the cell walls of—

F fungi

G bacteria

H plants

J animals

7 Traits that enable an organism to survive and reproduce in its environment are known as—

A mutations

B variation

C adaptations

D speciation

8 In the diagram of the light microscope below, which part regulates the amount of light passing through the specimen?

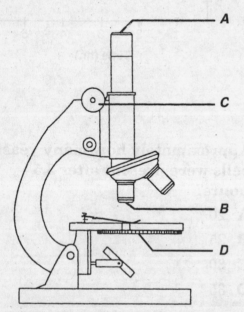

F A

G B

H C

J D

9 An organism with chitinous appendages and Malpighian tubules most likely eliminates carbon dioxide through—

A spores

B spiracles

C spines

D synapses

10 A frog dissection is represented in the diagram below.

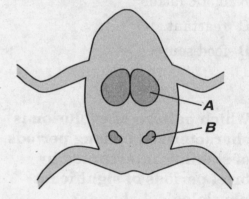

Which statement best describes the relationship of structure A to structure B?

F A is anterior to B.

G A is posterior to B.

H A is dorsal to B.

J A is ventral to B.

11 Which of the following is *not* a plant hormone?

A Auxin

B Ethylene

C Cytokinin

D Gibberellin

12 Prokaryotic cells—

   F contain membrane-bound organelles

   G contain large numbers of chromosomes

   H lack true nuclei

   J lack ribosomes

13 Chloroplasts and mitochondria are both believed to have been incorporated into eukaryotic cells through the process of—

   A photosynthesis

   B cellular respiration

   C phosphorylation

   D endosymbiosis

14 Viral activity is represented in the diagram below.

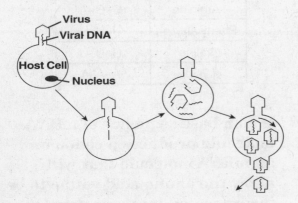

Invading the host cell enables the virus to—

   F increase its size

   G synthesize oxygen

   H obtain nutrients

   J reproduce

15 The modern theory of evolution includes Darwin's basic ideas, as well as the idea that—

   A large populations harbor variation

   B competition is an agent of natural selection

   C variation is the result of mutation and gene recombination

   D geographic isolation may lead to the evolution of a new species

16 In the early stages of development, the embryos of birds and reptiles resemble each other in many ways. These similarities suggest that birds and reptiles—

   F occupy the same ecological niche

   G evolved at about the same time

   H share a common ancestor

   J are both herbivorous

17 What process does the equation below illustrate?

   A hydrolysis

   B dehydration synthesis

   C pinocytosis

   D extracellular digestion

18 What do the root hairs of plants, inner cell membranes of mitochondria, and microvilli of the human small intestine all have in common?

F They are all associated with organelles.

G They all secrete digestive enzymes.

H They all create oxygen.

J They all increase the amount of absorptive surface area.

19 Which scientist is correctly paired with his contribution to biological science?

A Wallace—postulated use and disuse theory

B Watson—first to observe cells

C Lamarck—devised a system for naming organisms

D Fleming—discovered penicillin

20 Which concept is illustrated by the reaction shown in the diagram below?

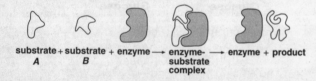

F Enzymatic specificity

G Protein denaturation

H Facilitated diffusion

J Oxidation-reduction

21 The diagram below represents a microscopic structure observed during cell division.

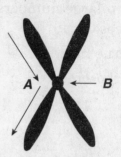

Which part of the structure is indicated by arrow *A*?

A Centromere

B Chromatid

C Centriole

D Cytoplasm

Base your answer to questions 22 and 23 on the chart below and on your knowledge of biology.

Amino Acid	mRNA Code
Leucine	C–C–A
Arginine	C–G–A
Phenylalanine	U–U–U
Valine	G–U–U
Lysine	A–A–A

22 Which base sequence of a DNA molecule produces a codon on an mRNA molecule that will allow the amino acid valine to be incorporated into a protein?

F G-G-T

G G-A-T

H C-G-A

J C-A-A

23 Which amino acid will be carried to a ribosome by a tRNA molecule containing the triplet code U-U-U?

A Valine

B Lysine

C Leucine

D Phenylalanine

24 The science of naming and classifying organisms is known as—

F taxonomy

G anatomy

H classification

J genetic engineering

25 Which diagram represents an organelle that contains the enzymes needed to synthesize ATP in the presence of oxygen?

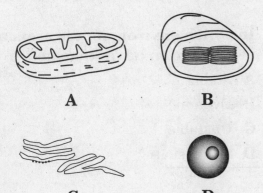

26 Which structures control the cyclic nature of menstruation?

F Scrotum and testes

G Pituitary gland and ovaries

H Uterus and fallopian tubes

J Corpus luteum and egg

27 The diagram below represents a human karyotype.

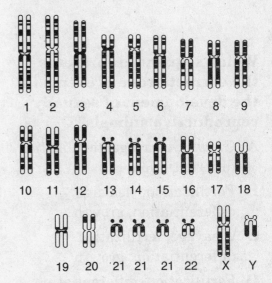

What do these chromosomes indicate?

A This is a female with Down's syndrome.

B This is a female with Turner's syndrome.

C This is a male with Down's syndrome.

D This is a male with Turner's syndrome.

28 Which phrase best describes a population?

F All the living organisms in a specific location

G All the nonliving materials in a specific location

H The maximum number of individuals of a species that a location can support

J All organisms belonging to the same species and living in one location

29 Which sequence represents the correct order of events in the development of sexually reproductive animals?

A Growth, cleavage, fertilization, differentiation

B Fertilization, cleavage, differentiation, growth

C Cleavage, fertilization, differentiation, growth

D Fertilization, differentiation, cleavage, growth

30 The technique illustrated in the diagram below is known as—

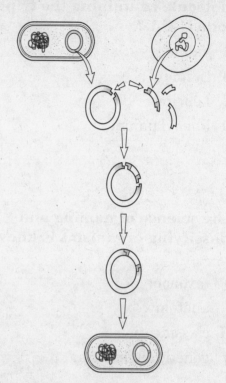

F genetic engineering

G cloning

H DNA amplification

J forensics

31 In which environment is asexual reproduction advantageous?

A Stable

B Dynamic

C Unstable

D Succession

32 Dormancy, food storage in roots, and seed production are—

F reproductive strategies in plants

G survival strategies in plants

H reproductive strategies in fungi

J survival strategies in fungi

33 Which English economist laid the foundation for the theory of natural selection?

A Wallace

B Darwin

C Cuvier

D Malthus

34 Which diagram represents an organism reproducing asexually through binary fission?

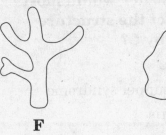

F

G

H

J

35 The diagram below shows a microscopic view of the lower epidermis of a maple leaf.

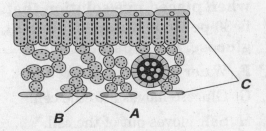

The cell indicated by *B* is—

A a guard cell

B a stomate

C an epidermal cell

D a nucleus

36 The first organisms to colonize bare rock are usually—

F fungi

G lichens

H grass

J weeds

37 The gene for tallness (T) is dominant over the gene for shortness (t) in pea plants. A homozygous dominant pea plant is crossed with a heterozygous pea plant, and two hundred seeds are produced. Approximately how many of these seeds can be expected to produce plants that are homozygous dominant?

A 0

B 50

C 100

D 200

38 What happens to the contents of a cell that is 90 percent water and 10 percent glucose when placed in a solution that is 80 percent water, 15 percent glucose, and 5 percent salt?

F Water moves into the cell.

G Glucose moves into the cell.

H Salt moves out of the cell.

J Glucose moves out of the cell.

39 Proteins and polysaccharides that are too large to move into the cell through diffusion or active transport move in by—

A exocytosis

B phagocytosis

C a proton pump

D an electron transport chain

40 In plants, energy is stored as—

F glucose

G lipids

H starch

J protein

41 The bond that joins two amino acids together is known as—

A a hydrogen bond

B a covalent bond

C an ionic bond

D a peptide bond

Base your answers to questions 42 and 43 on the diagram below and your knowledge of biology. The diagram shows some structures in the human arm.

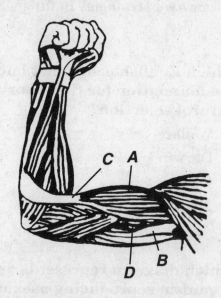

42 Which disorder would most likely affect the structure indicated by *C*?

F Arthritis

G Carpal tunnel syndrome

H Tendonitis

J Bone cancer

43 Which structure is an example of an extensor?

A *A*

B *B*

C *C*

D *D*

44 What is the principal function of structure *X* represented in the diagram below?

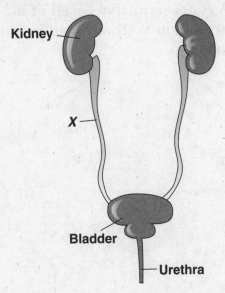

F Filter cellular wastes from the blood

G Transport nitrogenous wastes out of the body

H Storage of nitrogenous wastes

J Transport nitrogenous wastes from the kidneys to the bladder

45 Two abiotic factors needed by most animals for survival are—

A food and water

B predators and prey

C air and water

D soil and light

46 Recombinant DNA is presently used in the biotechnology industry to—

F increase fertilization

G treat infectious diseases

H treat genetic disorders

J decrease agricultural yields

47 The process of meiotic division in human females usually forms—

A one monoploid cell

B four monoploid cells

C one diploid cell

D four diploid cells

48 What type of life cycle is shown in the diagram below?

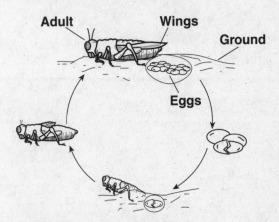

F Asexual reproduction

G Complete metamorphosis

H Incomplete metamorphosis

J Alternation of generation

49 A student wanted to investigate the effect of varying concentrations of auxin on plant growth. Bean plants were grown in soil in individual pots. Different amounts of auxin were sprayed daily on plants in different pots. The plants were grown at room temperature. At the end of one week, the plants were examined. As a control, the student should have used a pot that—

A was grown at 37°C

B did not contain a plant

C was not sprayed with auxin

D contained a tomato plant

50 The diagram below shows undisturbed sedimentary strata at the bottom of an ocean. A representative fossil of an organism is illustrated in each layer.

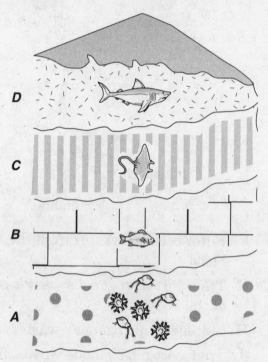

Which statement best describes a relationship between these representative organisms?

F All of the organisms probably evolved at the same time.

G Organism C evolved before organism A and after organism D.

H Organism B probably gave rise to organism C and organism A.

J Organism C is probably more primitive than organism D.

51 A collection of related hypotheses that have been tested many times is called—

A a theory

B a result

C an inference

D an observation

52 A scientific study showed that the depth at which algae was found in a lake varied from day to day. On clear days, the algae was found as much as six meters below the surface of the water, but was found only one meter below the surface on cloudy days. Which hypothesis best explains these observations?

F Light intensity affects the growth of algae.

G Wind currents affect the growth of algae.

H Precipitation affects the growth of algae.

J Air pressure affects the growth of algae.

53 A student is investigating the effect of different environmental factors on the growth of a certain species of bean plant grown indoors in soil over a period of thirty days. Which factor would function as a variable in this investigation?

A Species of bean plant

B Season of the year

C Amount of moisture

D Type of planting medium

54 Which laboratory procedure would be best to perform to determine the nutrient content of food?

F Boil the food sample in water.

G Apply pH paper to the surface of the food.

H Place the food sample in bromothymol blue.

J Drop Lugol's iodine solution on the surface of the food.

55 Based on the fact that a pumpkin contains many seeds, what can be inferred about the flower of a pumpkin plant?

A It contains many large anther.

B It contains many sepals and petals.

C It contains a large number of stamens.

D It contains large numbers of ovules.

56 Which of the following is an inference about earthworms?

   F Earthworms are hermaphrodites.

   G Earthworms evolved from flatworms.

   H Earthworms burrow through the soil.

   J Earthworms have a ventral nerve cord.

57 Which instrument was used in the eighteenth and nineteenth centuries and helped scientists develop the cell theory?

   A Ultracentrifuge

   B Gel electrophoresis

   C Light microscope

   D Electron microscope

58 Which indicator helps to make cellular components more visible?

   F Bromothymol blue

   G Methylene blue

   H Biuret solution

   J Benedict's solution

59 A food web is shown in the diagram below.

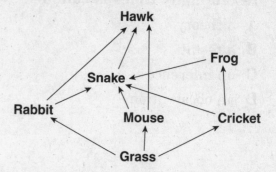

Which statement best describes a direct result of an increase in the frog population?

   A The hawk population will decrease.

   B The cricket population will increase.

   C The snake population will increase.

   D The rabbit population will decrease.

60 A student adds several drops of methylene blue to a sample of cheek cells. Which cell component would become more visible under low power of a compound light microscope as a result of this procedure?

   F Centromere

   G Mitochondria

   H Nucleus

   J Ribosomes

Answers and Explanations for Practice Test 2

PRACTICE TEST 2: ANSWERS AND EXPLANATIONS

1. **A** Limiting factors are abiotic and biotic factors that act on populations. Abiotic factors are nonliving environmental factors such as salt and water, which affect individual organisms within a population, regardless of population size. **B**, biotic factors, are limiting factors within the environment that are produced as a result of intraspecific and interspecific interactions. **C**, a reactant, is a substance involved in a chemical reaction. In this case, salt is not a food source, **D**.

2. **F** Gould and Eldridge proposed the theory of punctuated equilibrium as an alternate interpretation of the fossil record. Punctuated equilibrium describes the evolution of organisms as following a long course of time in which species changed very little. This period of stability, or stasis, is followed by short periods of rapid change. Species that cannot adapt to rapid changes become extinct. The ones that can adapt evolve into new species. Dynamic equilibrium, **G**, occurs when the number of births is equal to the number of deaths within a population. The climax community, **H**, is a community that will not be replaced by another unless the environment undergoes dramatic change. Homeostasis, **J**, is the maintenance of constant internal conditions.

3. **B** Homologous chromosomes are paired during metaphase I of meiosis. Separation of paired chromosomes during disjunction follows pairing and results in the formation of sets of double-stranded chromosomes

4. **H** The hydra is one of the smallest cnidarians, a relative of jellyfish. Hydrozoans have specialized tissues and an internal body cavity, but do not have distinct organ systems. Therefore, nutrients enter cells and wastes exit cells through diffusion.

5. **C** To determine the number of yeast cells present after 3.5 hours, find the point on the graph where 3.5 hours intersects the line graph. Follow that point horizontally back to the y-axis. Using this method, according to the graph, there were approximately thirty-five yeast cells after 3.5 hours of growth.

6. **F** Cell walls are structural features that are commonly found in fungi, plants, protists, and bacteria. The cell walls of each group are composed of unique structural molecules. Chitin a unique structural molecule found only in the cell walls of fungi, as well as the exoskeletons of many invertebrates.

7. **C** Adaptations are traits that allow a species to survive in its environment. **A**, mutations, are genetic alterations that may or may not lead to favorable characteristics or phenotypes. **B**, variation, is the number of different phenotypes within a population. **D**, speciation, is the development of a new species as a result of the accumulation of genetic variation that allows the species to adapt to new environment conditions.

8   J   Adjusting the diaphragm, **J**, changes the amount of light passing through the specimen. **F** indicates the ocular lens. **G** indicates the objective lens. **H** indicates the coarse adjustment knob.

9   B   Chitinous appendages and Malpighian tubules are structures that characterize arthropods, including insects. Spiracles are small openings or pores in arthropods that serve as points of entry for respiratory gases from the atmosphere. **A**, spores, are asexual reproductive structures produced by fungi. **C**, spines are modified leaf structures in plants that act to minimize water loss. **D**, synapses, are gaps that separate the terminal branches of one neuron from the dendrites of the adjacent neuron.

10   F   The head end of the organism is always the anterior end, while the tail end is always the posterior end. Because *A* is closest to the head, *A* is anterior to *B*.

11   B   Ethylene is not a hormone in the truest sense of the word, because ethylene is not produced in one part of the plant and then transported to another part where it exerts a long-term effect. Instead, ethylene is a gaseous growth factor that influences fruit-ripening, as well as fruit, flower, and leaf drop. **A**, **C**, and **D** are hormones that affect cell and plant growth and development.

12   H   Prokaryotic organisms are characterized by the absence of membrane-bound organelles, including true nuclei. The genetic material of prokaryotes floats freely in the cytoplasm.

13   D   Chloroplasts and mitochondria are organelles that have their own DNA. The DNA of these organelles is distinctly different from nuclear DNA. Scientists believe that these organelles have bacterial origins. The endiosymbiont model proposes that ancient bacteria were phagocytized, leading to the evolution of chloroplasts and mitochondria.

14   J   Viruses are not cells, and therefore lack the ability to grow on their own. The protein coat of most viruses allows them to penetrate cell membranes. Viral DNA is then added to the DNA of the host cell, which replicates the viral DNA along with its own.

15   C   The publication of Darwin's *On the Origin of Species* in 1859 predated modern understanding of the impact genes and mutation have on variation by almost one hundred years. Modern understanding includes Darwin's concepts of evolution as well as molecular explanations for levels of variations within populations. **A**, **B**, and **D** are Darwinian concepts.

16   H   The fact that birds and reptiles resemble each other during the early stages of embryonic development suggests that these two groups of organisms share a common ancestor. Beyond the initial stages of development, various structures such as limbs and tails are modified until they take on their characteristic adult forms, which are adaptations modified by environmental pressure.

17   **B**   Dehydration synthesis is a biochemical process in which simpler molecules are joined together to make larger molecules. During the process, one water molecule is evolved, or given off. Hydrolysis, **A**, is the opposite of dehydration synthesis. During hydrolysis, water is added to complex molecules, breaking them down into simpler ones. During pinocytosis, **C**, substances too large to diffuse through the cell membrane are taken into the cell in vacuoles. Extracellular digestion, **D**, takes place in a specialized organ or organ system.

18   **J**   Root hairs of plants, the inner membrane of mitochondria, and microvilli of the human small intestine, all increase the amount of surface area available for water absorption, cellular respiration, and nutrient absorption, respectively.

19   **D**   Alexander Fleming discovered penicillin while studying bacteria in 1928. In the 1940s, scientists discovered that penicillin was an effective treatment for a number of bacterial infections. Wallace, **A**, is co-credited with the development of the theory of natural selection along with Darwin. Watson, **B**, was one of the scientists who unraveled the mystery behind the structure of DNA. Lamarck, **C**, was the scientist who developed the theory of use and disuse as a mechanism for evolution.

20   **F**   This diagram illustrates the chemical combination of two specific substrates that takes place at an enzymatic site that fits the shape of the substrate molecules. At the end of the chemical reaction, the new product is released from the enzyme, leaving the enzyme and its active site unaltered. **G**, protein denaturation, results in the unfolding of proteins that inactivates them. **H**, facilitated diffusion, is the transport of molecules through a cell membrane against a concentration gradient using a carrier molecule. **J**, oxidation-reduction, is a type of chemical reaction in which electrons are passed from one atom or molecule to another.

21   **B**   A chromatid is one strand of a replicated chromosome. Chromatids are held together in an area called the centromere, **A**. A centriole, **C**, is an organelle found in animal cells that functions in cell reproduction. Cytoplasm, **D**, is the liquid medium inside cells in which organelles are suspended.

22   **J**   The complementary codon for the mRNA coding for valine, G-U-U, is C-A-A on the single strand of DNA. **F**, the complementary codon for G-G-T on the DNA, would be C-C-A on the mRNA, which codes for proline. **G**, the complementary codon for G-A-T on the DNA, would be C-U-A on the mRNA, which codes for leucine. **H**, the complementary codon for C-G-A on the DNA, would be G-C-U, which codes for alanine.

23   **B**   The codon on the tRNA (transfer RNA) is complementary to the codon on the mRNA. The complementary triplet code for U-U-U on the tRNA is A-A-A on the mRNA, lysine.

24   **F**   Taxonomy is a branch of biology concerned with naming and classifying life-forms.

25   **A**   The mitochondrion is the organelle that contains the enzymes needed to synthesize ATP during aerobic respiration. Chloroplasts, **B**, are flattened discs that contain photosynthetic pigments in the cell membrane. Chloroplasts are the site of photosynthesis. The endoplasmic reticulum, **C**, is a membrane-bound network used to transport proteins and lipids. The nucleus, **D**, houses the DNA.

26   **G**   The menstrual cycle is regulated by sequential secretions of the pituitary gland in the brain and the ovaries. The scrotum and testes, **A**, are male reproductive structures. The uterus, **C**, is the pear-shaped organ that supports the growth and development of the fetus. The fallopian tubes provide a pathway from the ovaries to the uterus and are the sites of fertilization. The corpus luteum, **D**, is a structure formed from the ovarian follicle that secretes progesterone, a hormone essential to the maintenance of pregnancy during the first months of gestation.

27   **A**   The karyotype indicates a male (sex chromosomes XY) with Down's syndrome, as indicated by three copies of chromosome 21. Individuals with Turner's syndrome have one X chromosome and are missing the other.

28   **J**   A population is comprised of all organisms belonging to the same species that are living in the same geographic location. A community is comprised of all of the organisms living in a given location, **F**. Abiotic factors are nonliving materials in a given location, **G**. Carrying capacity is the maximum number of organisms that an environment can support, **H**.

29   **B**   Fertilization is the necessary first step in the production of a new, sexually reproducing organism. Fertilization reestablishes the diploid condition, and is almost immediately followed by the mitotic cell division known as cleavage, thereby doubling the number of cells in the zygote. Three primary tissues—ectoderm, endoderm, and mesoderm—are produced through cell differentiation. These tissues give rise to specialized tissues and organ systems during the processes of growth and development.

30   **F**   The diagram illustrates the technique of genetic engineering, through which the DNA of two different organisms is spliced together. Cloning, **G**, is the process through which bacterial colonies grow many copies of genetically engineered DNA. DNA amplification, **H**, is made possible by polymerase chain reaction (PCR) technology and is used to make many copies of DNA. Forensics, **J**, is the application of science to law and criminology.

31 **A** A stable environment is an environment that experiences little change over a long period of time. Asexual reproduction is advantageous in this environment because of the conservation of energy that normally is expended while finding mates and producing gametes. **B, C,** and **D** all refer to environments that are changing and therefore require variability and adaptability.

32 **J** These are all plant strategies for surviving seasonal changes in moisture availability and temperature.

33 **D** Malthus's take on population growth and the inability of an environment's resources to keep up with population demands planted the seeds of what evolutionary biologists Darwin, **B,** and Wallace, **A,** would develop into the theory of natural selection. Cuvier, **C,** was the paleontologist who established the idea of extinction as a biological reality.

34 **G** Binary fission is a form of asexual reproduction that is characteristic of all prokaryotes and many protists. During binary fission, the cytoplasm and nucleus of the parent cell are divided equally to produce two new, identical cells. During budding, **F,** a miniature version of the parent organism grows on the body of the parent. At some point, the bud breaks off and grows into a full-size organism that is genetically identical to the parent. Many fungi reproduce through the production of asexual spores, **H.** The production of runners, **J,** is a form of asexual reproduction that is found in some plants, including strawberries.

35 **A** Guard cells are cells located on either side of the opening or pore called a stomata, **B.** Changes in water content of guard cells regulate the opening and closing of stomata. This affects the amount of gases and water vapor moving into and out of the leaf through the stomata. Structure C is an epidermal cell, **C.**

36 **F** Lichens represent a mutualistic relationship between a fungus and an alga. Lichens secrete enzymes that begin breaking down rock, thereby freeing the minerals in rock. These minerals become an important component in the soil that develops as organic matter is added to the minerals. **F,** fungi, is an important decomposer of organic materials, such as the bodies of plants and animals. **H,** grass, moves into an area after the first soils have been established. This stage usually follows the establishment of pioneer species like weeds, **J.** Pioneer species are species that are provided with enough soil to establish roots and therefore add organic matter to the developing soil. Pioneer species are quickly replaced by larger, more robust species.

37   **C**   Here's where the Punnett square comes in handy. When you set up your square, you find that crossing a homozygous dominant individual with a heterzygous individual produces an F1 generation that is 50 percent homozygous dominant and 50 percent heterozygous. Therefore, you can expect that of the two hundred seeds produced, approximately one hundred seeds will be homozygous dominant plants.

38   **G**   Substances will *always* flow from areas of high concentration to areas of low concentration. The concentration of glucose was higher outside of the cell than the concentration of glucose inside the cell. Therefore, glucose moved along the concentration gradient from outside to the inside.

39   **B**   Phagocytosis is a form of endocytosis, which is the process of moving organic materials into a cell by surrounding and engulfing foreign materials. *Amoebas* are protozoans that obtain food through phagocytosis. **A**, exocytosis, is the opposite of endocytosis. Exocytosis is the removal of material and wastes from a cell. **C**, a proton pump, moves protons into or out of a cell against the concentration gradient. **D**, the electron transport chain, moves electrons from one molecule or atom to another, thereby transferring energy.

40   **H**   Plants store energy in the form of starch. Starch is produced through dehydration synthesis of many glucose molecules.

41   **D**   Amino acids are joined together through the process of dehydration synthesis that produces a peptide bond. **A**, a hydrogen bond, is a weak chemical bond that links polar molecules together. **B**, a covalent bond, forms as the result of atoms sharing electrons. **C**, an ionic bond, forms between oppositely charged ions or molecules and are formed as a result of the gain or loss of an electron.

42   **H**   Structure *C* is a tendon and therefore susceptible to inflammation of the connective tissue that joins muscles to bone (tendons). Arthritis, **F**, is an inflammation of the joints. Carpal tunnel syndrome, **G**, is soreness and tenderness in the thumb and fingers caused by pressure on a nerve in the wrist. Bone cancer, **J**, is abnormal cell growth in bones.

43   **B**   Extensors are muscles that extend joints, allowing them to straighten. The tricep muscle that is indicated as Structure *B* is an example of an extensor. Flexors are muscles that cause limbs to bend at the joints. Structure *A*, the bicep muscle, is an example of a flexor. Structure *C* is a tendon. Structure *D* is the humerus bone.

44   **J**   Paired ureters connect the kidneys to the urinary bladder. Nitrogenous wastes in the form of urine are transported from the kidneys, which filter wastes from the blood, **F**, to the bladder, where it is stored, **H**, until it exits the body through the urethra, **G**.

45   **C** Abiotic factors are nonliving factors in the environment such as water, air, and light. Air and water are essential for the survival of most animals.

46   **H** Recombinant DNA results from the insertion of genes from one organism into the DNA of another organism. Recombinant techniques have allowed researchers to develop gene therapies and medicines that treat genetic disorders, such as cystic fibrosis and diabetes.

47   **B** Meiotic division always results in the production of cells that have half the number of chromosomes of the starting cell. Four monoploid cells are produced at the end of one cycle of meiotic division.

48   **H** Grasshoppers undergo incomplete metamorphosis during the course of their life cycles. Incomplete metamorphosis is characterized by developmental stages that are not tremendously different from each other. During incomplete metamorphosis, the juvenile or nymph has wings and is structurally very similar to its adult form. Butterflies are one group of organisms that undergo complete metamorphosis, which is characterized by developmental stages that are significantly different from each other. Alternation of generations, **J**, is a life cycle characterized by both haploid and diploid stages. The life cycle of plants follows the alternation of generation life-cycle plan.

49   **C** A bean plant grown under identical experimental conditions but that has not been sprayed with auxin serves as a control for this experiment.

50   **J** The principle of superposition states that in an undisturbed rock layer, the layers on the bottom are older than the layers on the top. William Smith was one of the first to notice that organisms in older rock layers were generally simpler or more primitive than the fossils found in younger rock layers. Therefore, because the rock layer containing organism *A* is on the bottom of the rock layer, you can infer that organism *A* is more primitive than the fossil organisms in the younger layers, provided that the rock column is undisturbed.

51   **A** A theory is a unifying explanation for a broad range of observations that has developed through extensive and exhaustive experimentation. Therefore, theories are generally accepted scientific principles. A result, **B**, is the end product of experimentation. An inference, **C**, is a conclusion that is drawn based on observation and scientific knowledge. An observation is information gathered from the environment using one or more of your sense organs.

52   **F** The layout of this experiment indicates that light intensity is the variable in this experiment, as changes in light levels influence the depth at which algae was found. There is no mention of wind, precipitation, or air pressure in the original experiment, so there is no way to know how these factors affected the results.

53   **C** Soil moisture content is the only variable listed. **A, B,** and **D** remain the same for all replicates in this experiment.

54   **J** Lugol's iodine solution is an indicator that turns blue-black in the presence of starch. **F, G,** and **H** are not procedures used to detect the presence of nutrients.

55   **D** The seeds of a pumpkin plant or any fruit develop from the ovules located inside the ovary of a flower. Therefore, the number of seeds present in a fruit is a reflection of the number of ovules present in the ovary of a flower.

56   **G** Because no one was around to observe the evolution of earthworms, one can only infer their evolutionary relationship to flatworms based on physiological and molecular similarities. **F, H,** and **J** are readily observable using one of more of your five senses.

57   **C** The light microscope was an invaluable tool used for ferreting out the truth about microscopic life. This led to pivotal discoveries about plant and animal cells and eventually to the development of the cell theory.

58   **G** Methylene blue is a stain commonly used to make cellular organelles more visible under a microscope. **F**, bromothymol blue, is an indicator solution used to determine the qualitative acidity or basicity of a solution. **H**, biuret solution, is an indicator solution used to detect the presence of proteins. **J**, Benedict's solution, is an indicator used to detect the presence of carbohydrates.

59   **C** Frogs act as primary consumers, feeding on crickets while also serving as prey items for both snakes and hawks. A significant increase in the frog population means that more energy is available for predators, such as snakes and hawks. Therefore, the population of these animals has the potential to increase with increasing frog availability. An increasing frog population spells bad news for frog prey, such as crickets. The cricket population will very likely decline as a result. The burgeoning frog population will not significantly impact the rabbit population.

60   **H** Methylene blue is a common stain used to make large cellular components such as nuclei more visible when viewed through a light microscope on low power. **F, G,** and **J** are cellular structures that are too small to be viewed using this standard technique.

PRACTICE TEST SCORING GUIDE

PRACTICE TEST 1

Total 60 questions _____ / 60 Correct

– 10 field test items _____ / 10 Correct

(3, 8, 11, 21, 24, 32, 40, 44, 48, 55)

Total 50 questions _____ / 50 Correct

0–30 = failing

31–44 = passing

45–50 = advanced

PRACTICE TEST 2

Total 60 questions _____ / 60 Correct

– 10 field test items _____ / 10 Correct

(4, 9, 13, 16, 27, 31, 40, 45, 52, 58)

Total 50 questions _____ / 50 Correct

0–30 = failing

31–44 = passing

45–50 = advanced

NOTES

NOTES

NOTES